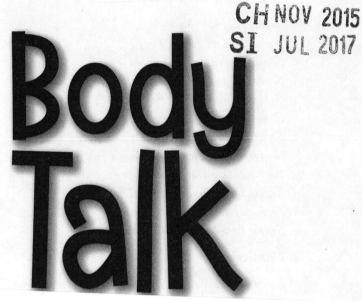

Body Talk

Other books in the growing Faithgirlz!™ library

The Faithgirlz!™ Bible
NIV Faithgirlz!™ Backpack Bible
My Faithgirlz!™ Journal

The Sophie Series

Sophie's World (Book One)
Sophie's Secret (Book Two)
Sophie Under Pressure (Book Three)
Sophie Steps Up (Book Four)
Sophie's First Dance (Book Five)
Sophie's Stormy Summer (Book Six)
Sophie's Friendship Fiasco (Book Seven)
Sophie and the New Girl (Book Eight)
Sophie Flakes Out (Book Nine)
Sophie Loves Jimmy (Book Ten)
Sophie's Drama (Book Eleven)
Sophie Gets Real (Book Twelve)

Nonfiction

Everybody Tells Me to Be Myself but I Don't Know Who I Am
The Skin You're In: Discovering True Beauty
Girl Politics
No Boys Allowed: Devotions for Girls
Girlz Rock: Devotions for You
Chick Chat: More Devotions for Girls
Shine On, Girl!: Devotions to Make You Sparkle

Check out www.faithgirlz.com

faiThGirLz!
2 corinthians 4:18

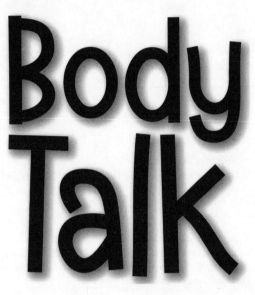
Body Talk

Nancy Rue

ZONDERkidz

ZONDERVAN.com/
AUTHORTRACKER
follow your favorite authors

We want to hear from you. Please send your comments about this book to us in care of zreview@zondervan.com. Thank you.

ZONDERKIDZ

Body Talk
Copyright © 2007 by Nancy Rue

Requests for information should be addressed to:
Zonderkidz, *Grand Rapids, Michigan* 49530

Library of Congress Cataloging-in-Publication Data

Rue, Nancy N.
    Body talk / by Nancy Rue.
        p. cm. — (Faithgirlz)
    ISBN 978-0-310-71275-6 (softcover)
    1. Preteens. 2. Girls — Psychology. 3. Girls — Health and hygiene. 4. Puberty. 5. Body image in adolescence. I. Title.
HQ777.15.R84 2007
613'.04242 — dc22

                                                                2007021354

Published in association with the literary agency of Alive Communications, Inc., 7680 Goddard Street, Suite 200, Colorado Springs, CO 80920, www.alivecommunications.com

Zonderkidz is a trademark of Zondervan.

Editor: Barbara Scott
Interior design: Sherri L. Hoffman
Art direction: Merit Kathan

Printed in the United States of America

---

14 /DCI/ 28 27 26 25 24 23 22 21 20 19 18 17 16 15 14

Contents

So we fix our eyes not on what is seen, but on what is unseen. For what is seen is temporary, but what is unseen is eternal.

—2 Corinthians 4:18

chapter one

What's
HAPPENING?

C ourtney stuck her face into the Doritos bag. It wasn't
because she was a freak for chips. She just didn't want anybody else at the slumber party to see that she clearly had no
clue what they were talking about.

"Getting your period is, like, way painful," Anna Adams said.

*What "period" did she mean? Surely not the kind at the end of a
sentence . . .*

"Have you gotten yours?" Kayla Cartwright said.

Anna shook her head. "No. I only just started wearing a bra a
month ago."

A bra? What for? Courtney snuck a peek at Anna from over the
top of the chip bag. *Holy smoke! She did have breasts. Where had those
come from?*

"Yeah, well, look what I started doing." Sydney Shaw pulled
up her pajama leg and exposed her calf.

"Dude — you shave your legs?" Kayla said.

Now that could be painful.

"Armpits too," Sydney said.

Sydney shrugged as if it were no big deal, but Kayla and
Anna nodded, wide-eyed, as if Sydney had just aged five years
and yet was still gracing them with her presence.

*What happened to the stuff we used to talk about at our sleepovers?
Dolls and stickers and the best way to surprise a creepy boy with a water
balloon. Since when had periods — whatever they were — and bras and body
shaving become the main topics of conversation?*

"Hey," Courtney said.

Her friends managed to drag their gazes away from Sydney's naked leg. Courtney held up a bag of Peanut M&Ms.

"Anybody want some candy?"

"No way," Anna said. "I'm feeling, like, totally fat. I'm on a diet."

"You're a stick!" Courtney said.

"Hello! Look at this." Anna pinched at the skin at her waist. Courtney didn't know what she was supposed to be seeing.

"I'm not having any either," Kayla said, waving off the candy bag. "Boys don't like fat girls."

"Who cares?" Courtney wanted to say. But Sydney shook her head at the Peanut M&Ms and patted her own rear, which evidently explained everything to Kayla and Anna, because they nodded solemnly.

Courtney popped a handful of candy into her mouth and wondered, *What is* happening *here?*

What indeed? Courtney consumed the entire bag of Peanut M&Ms herself, while, far into the night, her friends discussed cramps and bra styles and the best way to lose ten pounds in a day. When she got home the next morning, Courtney went straight to the full-length mirror.

Wow. It was true.

She *was* getting hair where she'd never had it before.

She *did* have little breasts budding from her chest.

Her hips were definitely wider than they had been the last time she'd looked at them ... which was when, exactly?

The truth was, she'd never spent much time gazing at her own body. But she knew none of *this* stuff had ever been there before. And what was that smell?

Courtney sniffed at her armpit and wrinkled her nose.

"EWW."

And this probably wasn't even the worst of it. She'd gathered from last night's discussion — while she was sorting the M&Ms

by color — that someday soon she was going to get the dreaded "period." She still didn't know exactly what it was, but it couldn't be good. Not if it involved embarrassment and cramps and all the other stuff her friends had described — based on what had been described to *them*.

Courtney's reflection in the mirror blurred as tears came that she couldn't explain. She didn't usually cry, but this was huge. She was transforming into somebody else right before her eyes — and she didn't know what to do about it.

now what?

You might be a little better informed than Courtney about the changes that are happening to your body or *will* be happening in the near future. But there's a lot to know about this young woman that you're becoming, and this book is here to help you

> understand what's going on inside the little-girl body that's changing into a mini-woman body;
>
> learn to love it;
>
> take super-good care of it;
>
> avoid bullying it; and
>
> become God-confident that it's the best body for you and your life.

But we can't leave Courtney crying in front of the mirror because she thinks she's turning into an alien. If you were there, standing behind Courtney and looking at her reflection with her, what would you say? Is there advice you'd give her? Or would you just hand her another bag of M&Ms because you feel the same way yourself, and you don't know what to do either?

Whatever you want to tell our Courtney, write it in the space below. There are no right or wrong answers, so be honest. If, as you read the rest of this book, you discover something that makes you change your mind about how to encourage Courtney, you'll have a chance to "talk" to her again in the last chapter.

Dear Courtney . . .

_____

_____

_____

_____

_____

_____

_____

Take a look around at your girl classmates at school, your Sunday school girlfriends, or your sports teammates. Do you see any two bodies that are *exactly* alike? No way, because absolutely every girl's body is different.

There's one way that they're identical, though, and that's in the fact that between the ages of eight and thirteen, female bodies go through more changes than at any other time in their lives (even more than in the first year when you went from wrinkled and chinless to dimple-kneed and adorable in just twelve months). All girls go through *puberty*, when they transform from flat-chested and smooth-as-pears to miniature women with

breasts;
new hair under the arms and in the pubic area (y'know, between your legs);
thicker, coarser hair, on the legs especially;
sweat that has a less-than-lovely odor;
wider hips; and
taller, maybe even heftier, bodies.

You may ask, "And this happens because . . . ?"

Every female's body is designed to automatically start producing two new hormones some time in the tween years (though later for some girls). Those are *estrogen* and *progesterone*. Estrogen causes all of the above. Progesterone, with some help from estrogen, causes and controls *menstrual periods*, which happen once a month. More on those later.

As if it weren't enough for all that to be going on, the arrival of these new hormones also leads to some emotional changes.

Mood swings: You've got the giggles one minute, and the next you're crying, all for no apparent reason. Your body is suddenly a stranger to you, and it's out of control!

Changes in your attitude about boys: Where once you were convinced they were all possessed by demons, or at the very least had cooties, you find yourself wanting to look cute for them. Or you secretly enjoy it when the one least likely to actually *have* cooties unties your tennis shoe for the forty-third time.

Whew. Isn't it good to know you're normal?

That Is SO Me!

Not everybody experiences puberty at the same time in their lives or in exactly the same way—which takes us back to the fact that God made everyone unique. The following quiz will show you where you are on the changing-into-a-woman journey. As you take the quiz, remember that you aren't "behind" or "ahead" of anybody else. You're right where YOU are supposed to be.

Which of these descriptions sounds MOST like your body right now? Not everything will match you exactly, of course, so pick the one that's closest.

Girl One: No hair has shown up yet in her armpits or between her legs (pubic area). There don't appear to be any breasts in her immediate future, and her waistline is the same as it always was. Her hips haven't changed either. As for the hair on her legs, she doesn't really see much. There's never anything on her underwear when she takes her panties off.

Girl Two: She's noticed some hair sprouting in her armpits and pubic area, and the hair on her legs has gotten thicker and coarser than it used to be. She may or may not be wearing a bra yet, but she does have little raised bumps or pointy little mounds that will someday be breasts. Her waist feels kind of thick, and her hips have spread so that sometimes she feels, well, fat. What's really different is that when she takes off her underwear, there's sometimes thick, clear stuff on them, or maybe a brownish stain.

Girl Three: She's had hair in her armpits and pubic area for a couple of months or more, and she's thinking she might want to shave her legs (if she isn't doing it already). She definitely has breasts which are round and pretty full, and maybe the area around her nipples has gotten darker. She actually has a real waist now, and it feels like her hips are finally in proportion to the rest of her body. Sometimes she discovers blood spots on her underwear; she might even be having periods.

What does that all mean?

If you're like girl one, you haven't started puberty yet. Remember that no matter how old you are, that's perfectly normal. Reading this book will help you be ready when it does happen—and then you can enjoy the fun parts more.

If you're like girl two, you're already in puberty, even though you haven't started your period yet. This stage is where most of the surprises happen, so reading this book can be way helpful in walking you through those. It can even be fun.

If you're like girl three, you're well on your way to young womanhood. In fact, you're probably getting used to the whole idea. Keep reading. This book will help you be the queen of your own body.

Here's the Deal

One more time, remember this: Whether you are girl one, two, or three, you are right where you're supposed to be right now! If other girls tease you because you need a bra about as much as you need dentures, or because you have more curves than a mountain road, they're showing their fears about their own bodies. Hang in there—you'll all be mature women some day.

Every girl experiences the same changes, but they can happen in different ways. All of these ways are perfectly normal.

Girls of different ethnic backgrounds start puberty at different times. For instance, the average African-American girl begins puberty just before the age of nine. The average white girl starts right before the age of ten. And remember, not everyone is "average."

Pubic hair comes in all different thicknesses and colors and grows at different rates. One of the first signs of puberty, pubic hair starts as straight, light-colored, fine hairs and grows in stages to the final darker and coarser curly hairs. Some of that depends on cultural background too. Asian girls, for instance, seem to have less pubic hair than other girls.

The "puberty growth spurt" starts at different ages for different girls. For some girls it seems to happen in a big way, while for others it isn't as dramatic. In this two- to four-year time period, girls put on weight and grow taller at a faster rate (as much as four inches a year) than before (two inches a year on average). The growth rate slows down by the time girls have their first period. Most girls reach their adult height one to three years after their first period. That adds up to about nine inches during the puberty growth spurt, but, again, some grow more and some grow less. It's all good!

Your face will probably change some during puberty too. The lower part gets longer and your chin juts out more. Your forehead gets wider. You'll actually start looking more like an adult than a

IT (Important Thing): If you want a peek at how tall you might be when you're fully grown, try this:

- Convert your mother's and father's heights into inches.
- Subtract five inches from your birth-father's height.
- Add your birth-mother's height to that.
- Divide that by two.

That should be close to your adult height.

kid, which is, of course, cool. Some girls' faces get sharper and more chiseled, and others' faces get fuller and more luscious. If it seems like your face is staying its little-girl self, that's okay too. There is nothing wrong with having a young-looking face.

One of the most bizarre things about puberty is that the bones in your feet start to grow before other bones. That means your feet will reach their adult size before the rest of you does. Since everybody won't end up being the same height, everybody's feet aren't going to be the same size now either. Forget about comparing shoe sizes or worrying that you're going to feel like Ronald McDonald for the rest of your life. It will all balance out before you stop growing.

Then, of course, there are your hips. During the growth spurt, your pelvic bones grow, and fat grows around them — giving you hips. They make your waist seem smaller, and when your breasts develop — ta da! — you have curves. The thing is, there are basically three different body types for those curves to grow into.

You're born with a body type already programmed in to develop during puberty:

Endomorph: round body with soft curves and a little more body fat (which is NOT a bad thing!)

Ectomorph: slim body with fewer curves and more angles (not a bad thing either!)

Mesomorph: muscular body with wide shoulders and slim hips (just as girl-like as the other body types!)

endomorph   ectomorph   mesomorph

Since your body type is part of the You package you came with, there is no reason to compare it to other girls' body types and every reason to love it as it is. Besides, the weight spurt and the growth spurt don't always happen at the same time. It's more like a seesaw: for a while you're adding pounds faster than you're adding inches; then for a while you're gaining inches faster than you're gaining pounds. Everybody's seesaw is moving at a different, personal rate, so there's no need to get hung up on feeling fat or thinking you're scrawny next to your friends. As long as you're healthy, let it be. You're growing into a specially made You.

Does it seem like your moods are always out of sync with your friends' moods? Do you sometimes feel like letting it all hang out in silliness, while one of your friends is stuck in a funk—or the other way around? Many of the roller-coaster rides your moods and feelings take during puberty are caused by the new hormones your body is producing. Hormones are way powerful, and they definitely affect emotions. Some girls (and some grown-up women) are really jolted around emotionally by their hormones, and others seem to ride right over them. It takes awhile for your body to adjust to those hormonal changes, so hang in there, and for heaven's sake don't think you're a total drama queen next to your best friend who never sheds a tear. Just how your moods bounce around—or don't bounce around—depends partly on the way you've always reacted to the things that happen around you. If you were born a sensitive baby, you're probably going to

IT: Don't be surprised if at times you're not even sure how you're feeling. During these years, you'll get to know yourself better and be able to figure out just what's going on with you. Once you do that, you'll be able to deal with your friends' ups and downs too.

be extra sensitive during puberty. If you've been a little toughie from birth, you'll more than likely be a little short-tempered in your puberty years — perhaps more rebellious than your weepier friends. If you've been laid back since day one, that will probably continue. Basically, who you are emotionally will seem to be magnified about a jillion times.

GOT GOD?

By this time, you might be wondering what you're going to do with all these changes. It can be confusing, weird — and downright scary! It's a good thing you don't have to go it alone. You've got God, who designed the whole process in the first place. Even if you don't particularly feel like *thanking* God for that right now, take a look at the help God offers:

God wants you to become a woman. And not just any woman, but one different from all others.

Sixty queens there may be, and eighty concubines, and virgins beyond number; but my dove, my perfect one, is unique.
— Song of Songs 6:8 - 9

God knows how strange and frustrating and often embarrassing and sometimes even painful the process of becoming a woman can be. God understands that it's a big deal. He's been hearing about it forever.

We have a young sister, and her breasts are not yet grown. What shall we do for our sister?
— SONG OF SONGS 8:8

God listens to you when you have complaints and doubts and fears about this whole puberty thing. After all, God even says there's nothing too small to pray about.

"Are not two sparrows sold for a penny? Yet not one of them will fall to the ground apart from the will of your Father. And even the very hairs of your head are all numbered. So don't be afraid; you are worth more than many sparrows."
— MATTHEW 10:29-31

Puberty's a lot to handle, and we don't have any choice about going through it! However, God never gives us anything to deal with that he doesn't also give us the tools for. Relax, enjoy the becoming, and remember that God has it all under control.

You're Good to Go

Since a huge part of puberty is wondering whether you're "normal," why not find out that you are? Through forming a "sisterhood," you and your friends can not only reassure yourselves that all of you are normal-for-you, you'll also be able to bolster each other up on the puberty path. You're always going to need a support group of women, so get started now!

What you'll need:

a group of friends who are about your age: this can be you and your best friend, a circle of four or five girls you usually hang out with, or a bunch that comes together because you all need to (God often arranges that!)

a place to meet for the first time

this book, in case questions come up that nobody knows the answer to

What to do:

Gather your group, maybe with some snacks on hand, and explain that since everybody's body is changing right now, you want to create a sisterhood, a safe group where you can share your experiences and anxieties and joys of going through puberty. Assure anybody who doesn't feel comfortable that she's not going to be totally shunned if she doesn't want to talk about this stuff.

Lay some ground rules: Whatever is said in the group isn't to be spread around (especially to boys!); no teasing; no comparing to each other.

Start with an activity to help all of you feel comfortable sharing personal stuff. Maybe everybody can tell about something embarrassing that's happened with bras, periods, or whatever. Perhaps you could read out loud from this book or take the quiz together or even just agree to get the group together when you have a question or a problem.

You don't have to meet on a regular basis. In fact, if you already hang out together, it will just come naturally. Whenever you do get together to talk, you might want to consider some of the following topics:

❖ Decide how you're going to deal with teasing from other people, especially boys. (You'll learn how in chapter seven.)

❖ Help each other get prepped for that first period. (You'll learn how in chapter three.)

❖ Compare notes on things like what bras are comfortable (chapter two), which razors are safe (in case anybody starts shaving), or who's doing what about smelly feet (chapter six).

❖ Most of all, agree to be there for each other if things get confusing or scary; make a pact to pray for each other always.

What this tells you:

Being part of a sisterhood tells you that you're not the only one dealing with all these changes — and that the changes themselves can actually be fun if you go through them with friends.

That's What I'm Talkin' About!

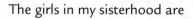

The girls in my sisterhood are

_____

_____

_____

So far we've helped each other with

_____

_____

_____

They're making puberty easier because

_____

_____

_____

chapter two

Breasts, Bras, and
OTHER GIRL THINGS

C ourtney wished for one of those saws she'd seen in cartoons. She wanted to cut a circle around herself in the floor and fall through. Away from Ferris Fox.

He was at that very moment working his way down the table in the cafeteria where she and her friends were *trying* to eat lunch. He ran his hand across each girl's back like he was dragging a stick along a fence. And after each one he announced whether she was "wearing."

"She's wearing," he said behind Anna. "Wearing," above Kayla's head.

Two more girls and he'd be at Courtney's back. She knew her face was already the color of the ketchup in the little paper cup on her tray — because she wasn't "wearing."

"Ferris, don't you have anything better to do?" Sydney said from across the table.

"No," said Anna. "For that, he'd actually need a brain."

Everybody at the table rolled her eyes, but nobody told Ferris to stop. By then, his hand was poised behind Courtney's braless back. There was only one thing to do.

Gritting her teeth, she said between them, "Touch me, boy, and you'll draw back a nub."

The table erupted in giggles, but Ferris could still be heard above them. Without even touching Courtney, Ferris said, "Definitely *not* wearing."

When he had sauntered off to continue his search for lingerie at another table, Anna leaned toward Courtney.

"Don't pay any attention to him," she said. "He's just annoying."

Courtney shrugged, but she knew her face was still ketchup colored.

"Besides, who cares if you aren't wearing a bra yet," Kayla said. "It's not like the biggest deal in the world."

"Whatever," Courtney said. But inside she was convinced that it *was* the biggest deal — at least in *her* world.

Here's the Deal with Breasts

Developing breasts and getting your first bra really is a big deal. It's one of the fist signs that you've started puberty, and it's the most obvious signal to other people that you're becoming a young woman.

That's a good thing. Having breasts means

you're developing a new, feminine shape;

you can wear a different style of clothes;

you might feel more grown-up; and

you *look* more grown-up, so anybody who knows anything will treat you less like a little girl.

Of course, there are challenges that come with those breasts:

Some people, especially boys (like that clueless Ferris Fox), may tease you because your new body means things are changing in their world too, and that makes them nervous.

You might feel like you're developing way ahead of the other girls or way behind them.

You may wonder if your breasts are normal, and it's hard to know since you don't actually see a lot of other girls' breasts to compare yours to.

You could have bra issues, like what size bra to wear, what style to pick, or how to get your mom to agree you need one.

Your growing breasts might actually scare you because you still feel pretty young, and you don't think you're ready to be a woman yet.

Relax. In this chapter we'll take a look at all those breast challenges so you can enjoy this part of becoming a mini-woman. Let's start with what God has to say about blossoming chests.

GOT GOD?

You mean God thinks about my breasts?

Uh, yeah. God created them, after all. As far as we can tell, God gave women breasts for a couple of reasons:

God sculpted Eve (and all women) to be attractive to men so the guys would want to marry and live their lives with them. The minute Adam saw Eve, he said she was now bone of his bones and flesh of his flesh. It doesn't get much more romantic than that.

God also gave breasts a practical purpose, which was to feed babies. Your breasts contain mammary glands, which produce milk when a baby is born. Not all women will have children or breastfeed them if they do, but the right stuff is there just in case. God actually made it pretty easy for moms when you think about it. No matter where moms are, the milk is always there for their hungry infants.

As beautiful and functional as God makes breasts, he also instructs us to keep them covered unless we're in private with our husbands (or a doctor when necessary). That just shows you how precious breasts are.

Feel free to thank God for this new shape your body is taking, and ask him to guide you in everything regarding it. Then you'll be ready to face the challenges one by one.

That Is SO Me!

Let's start with the issue of when your breasts develop and how fast. Take a look at your own chest and take this "Keeping Abreast Quiz."

Put a star (*) next to the description that sounds most like you. You'll need to know two words first:

nipple: the raised nub in the center of your breast

areola: the colored circle around your nipple

____ 1. My chest is still flat. My nipples are a little raised, but they always have been.

____ 2. A small, flat breast bud has formed under my nipple, sort of like a button. The areola is a little wider than it used to be.

____ 3. I actually have a small breast, not just a bud. My areolas stand out now.

____ 4. My areolas and nipples have formed a separate little mound on my breast. They're pointier than they used to be.

____ 5. My areolas and nipples aren't a separate mound. Everything is one smooth breast.

The description you starred tells what stage of breast development you're in. Look at the number you starred and read about your development stage below.

Stage One — *Pre-puberty*: You'll have breasts when your body is ready. There is nothing wrong with you. You're not late or behind. You're simply You.

Stage Two — *Breast Buds*: This is the very beginning of your future breasts. It's kind of neat, isn't it? Don't worry if they aren't exactly the same size or if they stay this way for a year or if they blossom into the next stage after a few months. It's all what's right for you.

Stage Three — *Developing Breasts*: The shape of your breasts now is very similar to what they'll look like when you're an adult, but they're smaller. Don't worry about a thing! Just enjoy wearing the cutest, most comfortable bra you can find (more on that later).

Stage Four — *Nipple and Areola Mound*: This is an interesting stage to watch on yourself because your breasts may stay the way they are in shape and just grow larger, or they might move on to the next stage. In fact, don't worry if you skip this stage completely. Some girls do. By now you're probably used to having breasts, so just keep enjoying being a girl.

Stage Five — *Adult Breasts*: Even though you aren't an adult yet, your breasts have fully developed. They might continue to grow in size, but their shape is a sign of your womanly self. Don't worry if they seem too small or too big. We'll talk more about loving your body later. For now, celebrate that these breasts are yours, and they're fabulous.

IT: There hasn't been any mention of how old you should be at each of these stages because it's different for everyone — EVERYONE! Besides, when you start to develop has nothing to do with how fast you'll develop or how long you'll be in each stage. Just be fascinated with the way God has shaped your body. If anyone says you're "behind" or "too bosomy for a girl your age" (like you could do anything about it!), you can say with a smile, "No. I'm right where God put me." Who can argue with that?

A few more things to know:

* As breasts grow from stage to stage, they can be itchy or sore or even painful. That's normal (bummer, huh?). Just like all growing pains, the discomfort will go away.
* A bump under the nipple when the breast is growing is not breast cancer. It's just part of the blooming process.
* Your breasts won't necessarily grow at the same rate. Don't worry if one's bigger than the other. They'll even out, although no woman's breasts are identical to each other. The difference is usually tiny.
* Some girls' nipples don't stick out but seem to sink in. Not to worry if yours are inverted like that. In case you've actually thought about it, you'll still be able to breastfeed a baby.
* A little occasional fluid out of your breasts is not unusual. Don't try to squeeze anything out, though. It just makes your breasts leakier.

Here's the Deal with Bras

Once your breasts appear, you'll probably start thinking about a bra if you haven't already. It seems like there's a lot to consider, so here are the answers to the bra questions most girls ask.

Q : When should I start wearing a bra?

A : There's no "should," but these are the reasons girls wear bras:
   * Their breasts jiggle when they're active.
   * Their breasts are sore, and the support helps.

✳ They don't like their nipples showing through their clothes.

✳ Everybody else their age is wearing them, and they just want to be like the group.

There is nothing wrong with any of those reasons (even the last one). This is a time of change in your life, and if a bra makes it easier and more comfortable, then absolutely you should wear one. A girl knows when she's ready.

Q: What if my mom says I don't need one yet, but I think I do?

A: Show your mom the answer to the question above. If she needs more convincing, be your most mature self and explain exactly why you're craving a little lingerie. If she still says no, try wearing a pretty cami or a tank top instead and ask her again in a month or so. If you don't nag, pout, or pitch a fit, she will respect your maturity and may decide you're ready for this step after all. Keep in mind that it's sometimes hard for moms to let their daughters grow up, so go easy on her.

Q: How do I know what size to wear? I don't get the numbers and letters thing.

A: Bras come in sizes like 32A, 34C, and 36B. The number is related to the measurement around your chest, called the *band size*. The letter tells the size of your actual breast, called the *cup size*.

Here's how to figure out yours. Measure with a tape measure while you're wearing no shirt or a very thin and close-fitting top.

1. Measure in inches around your rib cage right under your breasts. _____ inches.
2. Add 5 to that number: _____ inches. If this number is odd, add another 1. That's your band size. My band size is _____.

3. Measure around your body at your breasts, putting the tape measure at nipple level. My chest plus breast size is _____ inches.
4. Use the chart to determine your cup size.

Compare band size to the chest-plus-breast size	Cup Size
Band size is larger.	AAA
Measurements are equal.	AA
Band size is up to one inch smaller.	A
Band size is up to two inches smaller.	B
Band size is up to three inches smaller.	C
Band size is up to four inches smaller.	D
Band size is up to five inches smaller.	DD

5. Put your band size next to your cup size and now you know your bra size. Always try on a bra, though, because the style can make a difference in how it fits.

Q: Who knew there were so many kinds of bras? Help!

A: There are basically six styles:

Training—This bra can help you get used to wearing a bra or make you feel feminine (even if you barely have breast buds), but it won't "train" your breasts to be bigger, smaller, or perkier!

Soft Cup—This very comfortable bra is seamless and smooth and light. It lets your breasts look natural. If you feel "saggy" in a soft-cup bra or seem to be spilling out of it, you might need a bra with more support.

Underwire—Just like it sounds, this bra has a wire encased in soft fabric just below each breast. It keeps your breasts snug and lifted and doesn't let them bounce. It isn't uncomfortable if it fits right.

Push-Up—This is for girls with smaller breasts who want extra lift and shape. At this point in your life, a push-up bra is probably too sophisticated.

Sports—Whether you play sports or you're always on the move … or you just have to be comfortable, a sports bra is for you. It's like a very tight tank top cut off just below your breasts. It does flatten you out, but who cares?

Minimizer—If you should happen to have breasts no one else has caught up to yet (C cup or above) and you feel self-conscious, it's perfectly okay to choose a minimizer bra. It's designed to make breasts look smaller without flattening them out. Be prepared for the straps to be thick, and if you're way active, be sure you can really move with this bra on.

Q: Do I have to wash a bra some special way?

A: If you don't want your bra to fall apart or become like a piece of cooked pasta, you'll need to treat it with care. Even if your mom does the laundry, it doesn't hurt to take responsibility for your "foundation garments." (How funny is that old-fashioned name for bras?)

❋ To keep the elastic from wearing out, don't wear the same bra more than two days in a row.

❋ Your bra will need to be washed as soon as it has the first sign of sweat stains or body smell.

❋ Washing by hand in lukewarm water with a gentle detergent is best. If you do toss it into the washer, put it in a mesh lingerie bag and wash at the coolest setting on a delicate cycle.

❋ Never use chlorine bleach—bye-bye elastic!

❋ Don't put the following kinds of bras in the dryer: cotton, underwire, or bras with lace or embroidered trim.

❋ For any other bras, use a low heat setting.

IT: *Like Courtney, you may run into immature or just plain thoughtless people who feel like they have to tease you about your breasts, your bra, or your lack of either one. Who knows what's up with that? No size or shape breast is better than another, just like no eye color is the best to have. Magazines and movies and TV might insist that only huge-breasted women with tiny waistlines are beautiful, but they're wrong. So if someone teases you in the breast department, just remember: Ignore and take back the power to be yourself by simply walking away. You (and your breasts) are sensational.*

You're Good to Go

Whether you're an ultrafeminine princess, an on-the-go athlete, or somebody in between, it's important to feel like the girl you are right down to your undies. Why not start now by creating a special space for your "unmentionables." (Can you stand it that women actually referred to their undergarments as *unmentionables* even in the early 1900s?) Whatever you call your bras, panties, socks, camisoles, and anything else you wear under your clothes, have some fun making your collection special. See if any of the girls in your "sisterhood" want to get together to make sachets (see below).

What you'll need:

all your undergarments (clean, of course!)

a drawer or basket or whatever you keep them in

a piece of very You fabric to line it with (pink satin? wild print? cute plaid?)

a 5" x 5" square of fabric that is cotton, a cotton blend, or lace (something that won't block the scent of the potpourri)

a piece of ribbon or string about 6" long

¼ cup of potpourri, dried cinnamon sticks, whole cloves, dried lemon or orange peel, or dried rose petals

What to do:

Take everything out of the drawer or basket and set it aside.

Clean your drawer or container as necessary: vacuum it or wipe it out with a damp cloth. Even spray it with a fabric freshener if you need to.

Spread your You fabric out in your drawer or basket to cover the bottom.

Organize all your undies into piles—bras, panties, other (camis, tights, things like that).

Fold each item in each pile and give the pile its own space in your drawer or basket. If you're using a big drawer, you can even make dividers out of cardboard and place them under the fabric.

Make your sachet: Put your small square of fabric on a table or counter, pretty side down. Put your potpourri or dried goods in the center and gather all four corners together to form a sack. Tie it closed with your ribbon or string.

Place your sachet among your undies to keep the whole drawer smelling lovely.

That's What I'm Talkin' About!

My new undies drawer makes me feel _____

_____

_____

I think bras are _____

_____

_____

When it comes to bras, my friends _____

_____

_____

chapter three

Every
MONTH?

Courtney stood outside the bathroom and peered up and down the hall to be sure there were no little brothers prowling around. She didn't want to be harassed while she was on a fact-finding mission.

At least not *this* fact-finding mission.

Certain she heard her two younger siblings wrestling in front of the TV downstairs, Courtney slipped inside the bathroom and closed the door behind her. She was going to figure out this period thing once and for all. Her friend Anna had started hers that day — whatever it was — and Courtney felt like she couldn't stand another minute not knowing what all the other girls seemed to be experts about.

She intended to ask her mom — her being a female too — but when she'd gotten home from school that day, Mom was on the phone organizing ... something. Courtney was desperate. She'd just have to figure it out for herself.

She opened the door to the bathroom closet and dragged out the step stool so she could see the top shelf. Deep in the tunnels of her memory was a day when she was about five and had asked her mom what was in those blue boxes in the closet. Her mom had said, "That's mommy stuff," and the next time Courtney checked, they'd been moved up to the top of the closet out of her reach.

Now she was sure the mysterious "mommy stuff" was part of what was apparently "girl stuff," because she'd caught a glimpse of a smaller version of the blue box in Anna's backpack.

Standing on top of the stool, Courtney spotted two boxes. One was open and displayed small tube-shaped things in paper wrappers. She stuck one behind her ear to inspect when she got back to her room, and then she opened the second, larger box. It was full of what appeared to be little pillows each in a sealed pouch with no explanation printed on the box.

People sure didn't want anybody knowing what these things were. Courtney stuffed one into her pocket and examined the box.

"Four-Wall Protection," she read on the side of the box. "Exclusive technology actively prevents and neutralizes odor."

"I have to be protected against something?" Courtney said out loud. "Something that stinks?" Maybe she didn't want to know about this after all.

"Courtney?" she heard her mom say outside the bathroom. "You okay in there, Hon?"

The door opened, and Courtney almost fell off the stool as she twisted to look down at her mom. Was she going to be in trouble for snooping around in "mommy stuff"?

But the corners of Mom's mouth twitched, and she said, "The tampon behind the ear is a nice touch."

She put out a hand to help Courtney down. "Looks like it's time for some girl talk," she said.

Here's the Deal

Courtney's mom took a long time explaining "the period thing" because there's a lot to know. Just to be sure you get the whole picture too, we'll start with the basics.

The real word for "getting your period" is *menstruation*. What you're going to see when you start menstruating is a fluid that looks like blood coming out of your vagina (you'll probably see it on your panties or a piece of toilet paper). There may be from a quarter to a third of a cup of fluid over the course of three to seven days every month. The reason some girls get freaked out about it is because they have to keep that fluid from getting on their clothes (chairs, couches, beds, car seats ... you get the idea), and it seems like it would be a big deal. Anything new seems like a huge thing at first, but once you get used to wearing protection for those few days, it just becomes part of being a girl.

After Courtney got that part, she had about a million questions, and you probably do too.

Q: Why do we have to go through something that's messy and embarrassing? What's the point in it?

A: The point is that menstruation is part of the system in you that can produce babies—your reproductive system. Take a look at this diagram of a female's body:

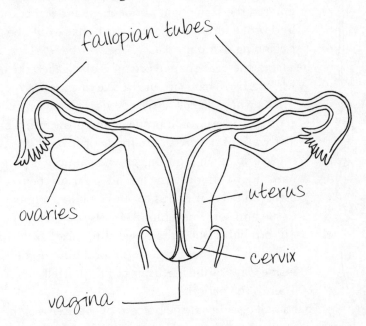

fallopian tubes

ovaries

uterus

cervix

vagina

Here's how all of that works:

The *ovaries*, those little almond-shaped organs, hold the eggs (also called *ova*) that you were born with. There are about 400,000 of them in there, some of which could help make babies someday (though not 400,000 of them!). The ovaries also make the hormones estrogen and progesterone that kick in at puberty and tell your ovaries to release an egg. One ovary lets one egg go one month; the other ovary lets an egg go the next month. That's called *ovulation*, and it happens about two weeks before your period.

The *fallopian tube*, which curves around and sort of reaches for an ovary, catches the egg as it's released from the ovary. It's only about as thick as a needle, so you can imagine how tiny the egg is. The fan-shaped part just over the ovary has fringe called *fimbria* that push the egg toward the tube where it's pushed along by little hairs. That takes about four days. If a guy's sperm entered the scene right about then, and it met the egg and broke through its outer shell, that would be the beginning of a baby.

The *uterus*, the pear-shaped organ, is also called the *womb*. Make a fist. That's about the size of your uterus. That's where an egg fertilized by a sperm (which is described above) would nestle in and grow into a baby. The walls of the uterus are made of strong, stretchy muscle so it can grow bigger when a mom is pregnant. Right after the egg is released from the ovary, estrogen tells the uterus to start building a lining of tissue and some new blood vessels to nurture the unborn baby. But if the egg isn't fertilized by a sperm (no baby), all that tissue and blood built up on the inside walls of the uterus has to flush itself out. Ta da! There's the period.

That small opening at the bottom of the uterus is the *cervix*. It opens up to release the fluid or to allow a baby to come out when it's born.

Both emerge from the same place, the *vagina*, that four- or five-inch-long passage from the outside to the inside of your body. Don't freak—it expands a *lot* for a baby to be born. God has all of that taken care of.

Q: So, what does a period look like? I mean, is it going to be like I'm bleeding to death?

A: A period is made up of three things: blood, the tissue that made up the baby-holding lining, and some mucus from your cervix and vagina. The blood gives it a red color, but it isn't all blood, so not to worry. It might be brownish at the beginning, and go to darker red, and then maybe back to brownish before it stops. If you see red clumps (clots), that's just part of the lining, and it's perfectly normal. The heaviest part of your period will be the first day or two, and then it will gradually taper off after that.

Q: But what do I do with all that stuff coming out of me?

A: That's where the blue boxes come in. Actually, they come in all kinds of packages, and they're called *feminine hygiene products* (just in case you're looking for them in the grocery store). It's much simpler than picking out a bra because you only have two basic choices.

Pads — Because they're so easy to use, most girls start with pads. A pad is made up of several layers of soft cotton in the shape of a dainty pillow. It has a sticky strip, so all you have to do is peel off the paper, press the pad into the crotch of your underwear, and it absorbs fluid. It feels a little funny at first, but you get used to it. There are different kinds of pads, but we'll keep it simple:

* *Maxi pads* are super thick in case you need that much protection the first few days. Then you can switch to *regular* (thinner) pads.
* Pads with *wings* wrap around the edges of your panties so you don't get side leaks. That can make you feel extra secure.

Whatever thickness you choose, we recommend the *body contoured* kind because they're shaped to fit your body and are the most comfortable.

❇ *Panty liners* or *panty shields* are very thin pads for the lighter flow of the last day or two.

Most pads and liners come individually wrapped so you can pop some in your purse or backpack. Be sure you have enough so you can change as often as you need to. Menstrual fluid does have an odor, so even when your period gets lighter toward the end, you definitely don't want to wear the same pad all day! Change about every two hours for the first half of your period and every four to five hours the second half.

A pad shouldn't be flushed down the toilet when you take it off because it will clog the plumbing. Fold it or roll it into a ball, wrap it in toilet paper or the wrapper many pads come in, and tuck it into the trash can. Most public restrooms have a metal container in each stall just for that purpose.

Tampons — These are the "tubes" Courtney discovered. A tampon is a cylinder-shaped, narrow strip of cotton that you insert into your vagina, where it absorbs the fluid before it even leaves your body. Since your vagina is muscular and flexible, it molds around the tampon to keep it from falling out. When you're ready to remove it, you just tug on the string that's left hanging outside your vagina, and it slides right out.

A lot of girls and women like to use a tampon because
✢ you can't even feel it if it's inserted right;
✢ it doesn't take up much room in your purse, backpack, or even your pocket;
✢ you won't have odor issues; and
✢ no one will be able to see it, even with a swimsuit or gymnastics outfit.

Not everybody uses them, especially in the early months or years of having periods, because

✛ the vaginal opening is small when you're young, so a tampon can be hard for some girls to put in;

✛ it takes some practice to insert one, and if you're already trying to adjust to having periods in the first place, it's less frustrating to wait a while; and

✛ some moms don't approve of them.

If Mom says no, you really have to respect that decision. If she says you might get sick (a rare condition called toxic-shock syndrome, which only occurs when women don't change their tampons regularly), have worse cramps (which aren't caused by tampons), or hurt you in some way (it's hard to hurt yourself with a roll of cotton), you could show her this section. Or you could just wait a while. Mom has to get used to you growing up too.

If you do get the go-ahead to try a tampon, here's how it's done.

1. Choose the kind of tampon you think will be best for you:

   Cardboard applicator — Made-up of two cardboard tubes, one inside the other; the outer one slides the tampon in, and the inner one pushes the tampon into place. They may get a little beat-up in your purse or backpack.

   Plastic applicator — This works the same way as cardboard and holds up better. It's also smoother than cardboard, but not as safe for the environment.

   No applicator — This is so small you can just push it in with your finger; good choice for beginners — no moving parts!

   Like pads, tampons come in different thicknesses (called absorbencies). It's good to have an assortment so you can use the appropriate absorbency for any point in your period. They come in extra absorbent, super, regular, slender, and junior. As you get to know your own periods, you'll find out what combination you need. You may use super the first two days, regular the next two, and slender for the rest of the time, or extra absorbent the whole time — or some other combination.

2. Read all the directions on the box before you start, and if you have any questions, ask for help from your mom, big sister, or another adult woman you trust. Then relax and take it step-by-step. If the tampon won't slide in easily, try again later. It isn't a failure if it doesn't work out the first time. A lot of girls are in high school before they've grown enough to use a tampon.

3. These are the usual things that trip girls up when they're trying a tampon for the first time:
   ❖ aiming the tampon straight up instead of at a slant; your vagina angles toward the small of your back.
   ❖ vagina is too dry; try some petroleum jelly on it, but nothing with a scent, which could irritate your skin.
   ❖ not holding the folds of skin open; you might just be pushing the tampon against skin.
   ❖ tampon is too big; try a smaller size or just wait until you grow a little. There's plenty of time, because you'll probably have periods until you're in your forties or fifties!
   ❖ it goes in but it hurts, which means it isn't in far enough. Push gently or start over with a fresh one.

Q : So, do I just keep all this stuff around all the time? I mean, who knows when my first period's going to surprise me?

A : To answer that question, why don't you take a quiz?

That Is SO Me!

These are all signs that a period will start in the near future. Circle the ones that are happening to you. (And remember, everyone's body is on a different timetable, so don't moan if you don't circle any! Your day will come.)

I'm older than eight.

My stomach is puffy and bloated.

I'm in breast stage three.

It's been about two years since I developed pubic hair.

Sometimes I see white sticky stuff in my underwear.

I have the munchies.

I have a lower backache.

My breasts are tender and swollen.

I'm crankier or weepier than usual.

I suddenly have pimples!

I'm tired and kind of sluggish.

If you circled at least five of the eleven signs, you'll want to be prepared with supplies at home and at school. There's no way to tell if it will be tomorrow or more than a month from now, but you'll feel more secure if you have it together. Besides, who knows when a friend will be caught padless? We girls are all in this together.

IT: You'll probably hear a lot of things about periods that just aren't true. These are some of the common whoppers that have been around since Eve got her first one:

Menstrual blood is poisonous. No way. It's made by your own body.

A boy can tell by smelling your breath that you're on your period. What? No, he cannot.

A dentist can tell you're on your period. Nah. And besides, if he or she could, who cares? This is a professional person who isn't going to announce it in the waiting room.

You can't go swimming if you're on your period. Why not if you're wearing a tampon? Now, a pad would be a problem because it's like a sponge. You get it.

A tampon can get lost up in your body. Not gonna happen. The only place it could go would be through your cervix into your uterus, and its opening is about the size of a match head!

You shouldn't wash your hair when you're on your period. There's no better time to stay clean and looking your best. It makes you feel better on bloated days.

Just remember: If you can do it when you're not on your period, you can do it during your period.

So far we've made having your period sound pretty easy, and it is most of the time. The few things that can bum you out—cramps, PMS, bloating, and irregular periods—are usually simple to fix.

Cramps—Cramps are caused by the tightening of the uterus muscles. Nobody knows exactly why some girls have pain before and during their periods and others don't. Usually it's a mild, uncomfortable lower stomachache, but one out of ten girls gets sharp pain that makes her want to curl up in a ball for the day. Other girls never have any discomfort at all (lucky!). If you're one of the unlucky ones, this should help:

Put some heat on your tummy—a heating pad, an herb pack you put in the microwave, or anything that will help your muscles relax.

Do some gentle stretches, like reaching down to touch your toes or sitting on your heels and lowering your forehead to the floor with your arms stretched out on the floor in front of you.

Be sure to get to bed on time, eat healthy (see chapter five), and drink plenty of water (not soda).

If all of that doesn't help, *ask your mom* for a mild pain reliever like ibuprofen (not aspirin). Ask to see a doctor for severe cramps that interfere with your activities. Your period doesn't have to be a time of suffering.

PMS—When a girl is crabby or snappy, you hear people—even guys—joking about PMS. Like everybody (including them) doesn't get like that once in a while! *PMS* stands for "premenstrual syndrome" and is a combination of symptoms that affect some girls the week before their period. It can include

feeling (and being) puffy and bloated;

wanting to eat everything that isn't nailed down, especially sweets and REALLY especially chocolate;

being crabby and irritable or feeling on the verge of tears;
ready to hug anybody (even your brother) one minute and
    ready to smack those same people (especially your
    brother) the next; and
needing to take a nap an hour after you just got up
    from one.

Although not everybody experiences PMS, the symptoms
are real—not all in your imagination. It's caused by the drop in
estrogen just before your period. Estrogen makes you feel happy,
so when it isn't there, you're likely to feel pretty down—physically
and emotionally. You don't have to be Susie Sunshine, but PMS
doesn't mean you get to be the Wicked Witch of the West and
everybody else just has to deal with you, either. There are things
you can do to help yourself be easier to live with for everybody,
including yourself:

Get some fun exercise.
Eat healthy carbs for snacks before your period and for
    the first few days. (See chapter four for ideas.)
Don't eat much sugar or drink caffeine. Do eat lots of
    veggies, whole grains, and nuts.
Get at least eight hours of sleep a night.
Talk to somebody who will understand about your
    feelings.
You might also try spending some time alone or doing
    quiet things.
Be nice to yourself during your alone time. Hot bubble
    bath? Soft music while you read your favorite book?
    Curl up with your cat? Just remember that being nice
    to yourself doesn't mean eating a whole package of
    Oreos.

Bloating—Feeling like the Pillsbury Doughboy? That puffy
look and feel in your lower abdomen is your body holding onto
fluid. You might even feel like an inflatable toy in your face, fingers, breasts, and feet. It will go away once your period starts, but
in the meantime here are some things you can do:

get some exercise;

cut back on salt and salty foods (yeah, that's right, chips, fries . . .), especially two weeks before your period;

eat meat, fish, poultry, whole grains, and leafy green veggies *instead of* junk food, fast food, and soda;

drink lots of water to flush out the fluid your body is hoarding like treasure; and

for bloated breasts, try a sports bra or other snug bra to make them less tender.

Irregular periods — Period one month, none for the next two, then two a month can be annoying, but that isn't unusual in the first few years. Keep supplies handy all the time until things settle into a regular rhythm, which is usually a period every 26 to 37 days. You keep track of your periods from the beginning of one to the beginning of the next. There are other causes of irregular periods, but here are some things that can cause your body to get out of balance (and some suggestions to keep it in balance):

Eating a lot of junk food (or not enough veggies and good protein) or going on fad diets. Read the "Table Talk" chapter and eat better.

Moving or visiting a new place. Give yourself a chance to adjust slowly. You don't have to feel right at home the first day.

Gaining or losing weight too fast. Eating right helps there. If your doctor says you need to lose weight for your health, take it "slow and healthy." No crash diets!

Being upset. Talk out your issues with an adult you trust. Write in a journal about stuff that bothers you. Be sure you have enough downtime to play, daydream, and just veg. Don't let resentments build up, and be sure to go to God with everything.

Being sick or getting hurt. Just know that any kind of trauma to your body may affect your period, and simply concentrate on your healing. Things will right themselves again.

Getting too much exercise. Didn't think that was possible? If you are pushing yourself to the point of exhaustion on the playing field and your periods stop, your body is trying to tell you to back off some when you feel heavy fatigue or pain. Your body is still growing—it isn't ready for a marathon yet!

Not getting any exercise. Couch potatoes often have whacky periods. Get up and get moving. The "Confessions of a Couch Potato" chapter will help you with that.

Irregular periods are the ones that catch you off guard. If you start yours when there are no supplies available, don't panic. You can improvise:

Use folded toilet paper, tissue, or paper towels to make a pad to slip into your underwear until you can get to the real thing.

If you're in a public restroom, look for a coin-operated machine. No money? It's okay to ask that woman washing her hands if she has change. No woman wants a fellow female to be without the right stuff; we've all been there.

If blood has gotten on your clothes, tie a sweater, jacket, or shirt around your waist and head for the nearest place to get a pad (school nurse's office, for example). If you have time, you can do the sweater-around-the-waist trick, take off your stained pants or skirt, wash it in cold water in the sink, and dry it with the hand blower.

IT: Don't spend a lot of time worrying that you're going to end up walking around with blood on your clothes, totally clueless unless somebody tells you. That doesn't usually happen. You'll probably feel something wet and sticky before it ever gets on your clothes. Most girls don't bleed enough right at first for it to seep through. Just keep a pad in your purse or backpack, pay attention to changes in the way you feel, and relax. If it does happen, you'll have a great story to tell at the next sleepover!

GOT GOD?

Some women call periods "the curse," a nickname which might go back to biblical times. In Leviticus 15:19–23, you can read about the rules for a menstruating woman:

> Anybody who touched her was considered unclean until evening.
>
> Anything she sat on or lay down on — anything she *touched* — wasn't to be touched by men, or that would make them unclean. (You didn't want to be "unclean" in those days; it meant you had to stay away from anything sacred, like the temple, until you went through a ritual to be cleansed, which wasn't just a matter of washing your hands.)
>
> Once a girl started having periods, no man except her husband could touch her again, ever (not even her father).

There were separate places for women to go when they were having their periods to keep them from touching anybody else in their "uncleanness."

You don't have to worry about being confined to the garage because you're "unclean" for seven days every month. Still, amid the cramps, and the worrying about bleeding on your favorite jeans, and the pads you're sick of by the fifth day, having periods can feel like somebody's cursing you.

But menstruation is just part of the amazing system God created for the nurturing of babies before they're born. Girls used to get married and have babies when they weren't much older than you are, so it probably made a lot more sense long ago to have periods at a young age. It's hard for you, at eight or ten or twelve, to think of it as a blessing for a baby you aren't going to have for years!

That means if you aren't going to let it feel like a "curse," you'll need to develop a positive attitude. God understands that periods can be a bit of a nuisance, but God obviously wants you to see that, overall, being a woman is a beautiful thing.

Read through the Song of Songs, which is a very short book in the Old Testament. It may seem bizarre at first, with some guy talking about how his lover's hair reminds him of a flock of goats coming down a mountain. But it's really a love poem showing how much God loves you, just the way a groom loves his bride. You might not be able to relate to God saying your teeth are as beautiful as a flock of sheep and your cheeks are like two halves of a pomegranate, but you can certainly think of this verse when you're feeling a little bit cursed. God says,

> "Arise, come, my darling;
> My beautiful one, come with me."
> — SONG OF SONGS 2:13

It sort of makes the cramps and the bloating worth it, doesn't it?

Even if you've already started having periods, it's probably all still new to you. And if you haven't started, you might be a little nervous. Even if you're thinking, "No, bring it on!" this "memories" activity might be fun for you.

With one or more women you're comfortable talking to, have a little informal gathering to find out what memories they have of getting their periods when they were tweens or teens. It can be a time for laughing — big time! — and for being reassured that every girl has been there — and survived. Besides, as we've said, we women need to bond on things men just can't understand.

What you'll need:

One, two, or three (at the most) adult or older-teen women you feel really comfortable talking to about things like puberty. It could be just your mom, or your mom and big sister and aunt, or your mom and her best friend, or your best friend's mom and the two of you — any combination you want. Maybe each girl in your Sisterhood would like to bring her mom. Some snacks would be good too. Something healthy or very girlie. Chocolate is almost always appropriate!

What to do:

Get together in a private place where you won't be interrupted (or spied on!) by any males. Your mom might want to get your dad's help with that part. Thank her/them for being there with you and then ask, "Will you share what it was like when you got *your* first period?" Be ready with some other fun questions too:

What was your most embarrassing period moment?
What did your mom tell you about getting periods and
    breasts and other girl things?
Do you have any advice for me about changing into a
    young woman?

Get out the snacks and celebrate that you are women. Don't forget to thank them/her for being there for you.

What it tells you:

The other women in your life have been through what you're experiencing. They understand. You aren't alone. You can go to them when you have questions or are just having a blue day and won't have to be embarrassed. You are part of a sisterhood that is there for you.

What to do now:

Thank God for their wisdom. Expect to feel less embarrassed next time you go to one of them with an issue. Don't be surprised if they treat you like you're just a little bit older — like you're one of them!

That's What I'm Talkin' About!

I heard some funny stories at our time together, like

_____

_____

_____

I found out I'm not the only one who's felt _____

_____, because I heard stories like

_____

_____

_____

After talking to her/them, I feel _____

_____

_____ _____

chapter four

Confessions of a
COUCH POTATO

Courtney had on the yellow bra today (the pink, blue, and white ones were nestled in her special lingerie drawer). And she had just tucked her ready-for-my-period kit into the bottom of her backpack that morning — complete with pads, clean panties, and a stain-remover stick. She was feeling pretty good about this whole turning-into-a-woman thing as she reached up to tuck her backpack into her cubby hole on the top shelf.

"EWW," somebody said.

Courtney lowered herself from her tiptoes and saw Valerie, the new girl, staring at Courtney's middle. Courtney tugged down at her shirt, which had crept up to expose her belly when she'd gone for the cubby hole.

"What?" Courtney said. "What's 'EWW'?"

Valerie wrinkled her nose. "You have muffin tops."

"Nuh-uh," Courtney said. "I don't have *any* food."

"No, silly." Valerie pulled up Courtney's shirt enough to let her tummy peek out. "The way your fat sticks out over the top of your jeans. That's called muffin tops."

Courtney yanked her shirt back down. "Hello-o! — Rude!" she said.

"Whatever," Valerie said. "Stay in denial if you want."

As soon as she could, Courtney escaped into the girls' restroom and, after making sure she was alone, stood in front of the mirror and pulled up her shirt.

Wow. Valerie was right. The flesh spilling out *did* look like the top of a muffin puffing out from the little paper cup.

"I'm fat," she said out loud.

Just then the door swung open and Anna and Sydney swept in. Courtney quickly covered up her belly.

"Whatcha doin', Court?" Anna said.

"Do you guys think I'm fat?" Courtney said.

Sydney bulged her eyes. "What? No way." She planted herself in front of the mirror and lifted up her top. "Now *this* is fat."

"Right," Courtney said. She could see Sydney's ribs.

Anna was looking at her, arms folded, brow wrinkled. "I'm not saying you're fat, Court, but you could probably use some exercise."

"You mean, like work out?" Courtney could feel her own brow drooping into folds.

"You could come out for soccer with us," Anna said.

"I hate sports!" Courtney wailed. "I stink at them!"

"So go skating with us Saturday," Sydney said.

"I don't skate that well."

Anna rolled her eyes. "Then quit complaining about being fat."

Courtney did. But all she could think about for the rest of the day were her muffin tops.

Here's the Deal

Let's get one thing straight before we start talking about getting Courtney — and maybe you — up and moving around. In this chapter we will encourage you to exercise so you will be healthy and strong — *not* so you will lose weight and look like a starving model. Before we go any further, read and remember these three things:

Unless a *doctor* says you need to lose weight for your
    health, it is *not* good for you to go on a weight-loss
    program at this point in your life. Although exercise
    may trim you down some, that should not be your
    goal. Your goal is to be as healthy as you can be,
    which is something we'll explore more in the pages to
    come.
As you learned in chapter one, your body is growing fast
    right now in two ways: height and weight. They prob-
    ably won't both happen at the same time, so you may
    find yourself feeling chunky at some point until your
    height growth catches up to your weight growth. (Just
    as you might go through a period where your weight
    growth hasn't caught up to your height growth and
    you are sure you look like a stick of bamboo.) *Do not
    worry about it!* If you eat healthy (read chapter five)
    and get good exercise (which is what this chapter is
    about), everything will balance out and you will be
    the lovely young woman you were meant to be.
Very few girls look like models and actresses. In fact,
    some of *them* don't even look like their pictures.
    Most photos are "fixed" by computers to smooth
    out "flaws." Even if the girls *are* bone thin with large
    breasts, they only make up a very small portion of the
    female population. The rest of us are gorgeous too,
    no matter what our shape. Get used to loving your
    body just the way it is on any given day. Love it so
    much you want to take care of it. After all, God made
    your body so you would take care of it.

GOT GOD?

News flash: Your body isn't really "yours." It belongs to God, and God has trusted you with it. Your job is to take care of it so it will be in the best shape possible for the work God has given you to do and so you can enjoy the gifts he gives you.

Think of it this way: If God gave you his personal bicycle to use, wouldn't you make sure you kept it running right and looking good — and be extra careful not to smash it up? Who wants to go to God with something of his that's all messed up because you just sort of let it go? That's the way it works with your body.

The Bible gives us the perfect verse to help us, and it's one you'll hear a lot as you get older:

Do you not know that your body is a temple of the Holy Spirit, who is in you, whom you have received from God? You are not your own; you were bought at a price. Therefore honor God with your body.

—1 CORINTHIANS 6:19-20

Exercise is one of the most important ways you can keep your "temple" in great condition. Give yourself a hug and let's go for it.

Just to get you pumped up, here's what exercise does for you. Exercise

- gives you energy and staying power so you can do all the cool things you want to do;
- helps you sleep;
- makes your muscles stronger and more flexible (which not only feels great but looks great on you);
- makes your eyes sparkle and your skin glow;
- builds your confidence; and
- keeps you from getting all bummed out.

Before we figure out how much exercise you personally need and what kind will work for you, let's find out where you are now.

That Is SO Me!

Under each question, pick the answer that comes closest to describing you. There are no right or wrong answers, so be honest.

I would rather
- a. play on a sports team.
- b. do gymnastics or cheers in the backyard with my friends.
- c. read a book on a porch swing.

If I could have a new, top-of-the-line item, it would be
- a. soccer cleats, a basketball hoop, or a softball glove.
- b. a bike, inline skates, or snorkeling gear.
- c. an iPod, a cell phone, or a digital camera.

continued on next page...

If my friend's family invited me to go on a daylong hike with them, I would
   a. be totally jazzed.
   b. say yes, but wonder if I could actually hike for a whole day.
   c. say no and wish they'd invited me to a movie marathon instead.

If we had to run a track in PE, I
   a. wouldn't be able to talk because I'd be running so hard.
   b. would be able to talk but not sing because I'd be running.
   c. could probably sing a whole musical because I'd be strolling.

When I'm exercising my favorite way, I think about
   a. winning or beating my own personal best.
   b. what a blast I'm having.
   c. um—I don't have a favorite exercise.

If you had mostly a's, girl, you are a serious athlete, and you like competition. You probably get plenty of exercise. Good for you for giving your body a good workout on a regular basis. Be sure to let an adult know if you ever experience any of these things while you're playing or practicing: pain, nausea, dizziness, or sudden major tiredness. It could mean you're working your body too hard. Otherwise, as long as exercise is always fun for you, keep doing what you're doing.

   If you had mostly b's, exercise is a total joy when it's something you can do on your own or during free time with your friends or family. Great fitness plan! Be sure you get some of that physical activity every day, and keep on enjoying it the way you do.

   If you had mostly c's, you don't get your body moving on a regular basis. Whether it's because you think you're a klutz when you try to play sports, you feel too sluggish and tired to be active, or somebody has made fun of you for the way you move, exercise isn't your favorite thing, is it? That's not your fault, and you know what? You don't have to be a soccer star or even feel all that graceful on a pair of skates to enjoy some kind of activity. Let's see if we can find something fun for you in this chapter—something that will get your heart rate up and speed up your breathing to get you healthier. You only have to do it twenty minutes a day, three times a week, but if you discover your personal exercise thing, you'll feel so good you'll want to do it more.

IT: Always be safe in any kind of exercise activity. Always stretch before you start. If you're biking, inline skating, or skateboarding, wear a helmet and knee pads. If you're playing basketball, wear high-tops. If you're practicing a sport on your own, wear the same protective gear as when you're with your coach. If you get hurt today, you won't be out there having fun tomorrow.

Here's the Deal

Now, on to your personal fitness plan ... Even if your schedule is already packed with sports and lessons, read these steps. You may find a small change you want to make so your exercise program can be even safer, healthier, and more fun.

Step One — Decide that you're going to do some kind of aerobic exercise at least twenty minutes a day, three days a week. That's the very minimum. The more you do, the better for your body ... as long as you don't feel sick or injure yourself. If you aren't sure you can make that promise to yourself, tell a grown-up what you want to do and ask that person to help you stay with it. Putting it in writing and posting it where you can see it will really help.

Step Two — Choose an activity (or several, so you don't get bored doing the same thing). Be sure your chosen activity

is *aerobic*, which means it will increase your heart rate and make you breathe harder than usual. Twenty minutes' worth is best, and a good rule of thumb is that while you're exercising, you should be able to talk fairly easily but not sing a song. Riding a bike, walking a dog, and dancing to fast music can all be aerobic. Doing one cartwheel, playing a video game, and walking from the TV to the refrigerator are not!

is something that *fits your personality*. If you like to compete, and you think games with teams and rules are fun, definitely play a sport. If you're a free spirit, pick an individual activity like bike riding or skating or swimming. If you are the happiest when you're hanging out with your friends, select something you can all do together that doesn't have a lot of rules and structure. That could be anything from shooting baskets in your driveway to organizing a skating party in your cul-de-sac. If you're a curl-up-with-a-book girl, find something practical that doesn't even seem like exercise. Can you walk to the library? Play backyard games with your little brothers and sisters to give your mom a break?

fits into your family's lifestyle and schedule. You might decide you want to ice-skate three times a week, but if the rink is on the other side of town and your mom is already spending ten hours a week chauffeuring everybody around . . . you get the idea.

Step Three — Set a goal for yourself. Make it something you can actually do but that isn't so easy it doesn't challenge you and give you a sense of, "Hey, I did that!" Be sure you'll be able to tell if you've reached your goal. If you say, "I want to be able to skate longer," that doesn't tell you when you're there. "I want to be able to skate for thirty minutes without having to sit down because I'm tired" will let you know when you can celebrate. Here are some examples of good fitness goals:

Swim the whole length of the pool three times without stopping.

Stay in the whole soccer game without getting too tired to play.

Ride my bike to school for ten school days in a row instead of asking my mom to drive me.

Play two straight hours of nonstop hopscotch for the neighborhood record.

If you don't have trouble getting yourself to exercise, let your goal be something wild like doing twenty cartwheels in a clown suit.

Step Four — Set up a fitness schedule for yourself. Maybe you already have one (you practice with your team several times a week, for example). Look for details about setting up a schedule in "You're Good to Go" below. It usually takes two weeks for something new in a person's life to become a habit. Until then, it's good to have a written plan you can see every day to remind yourself. "Today's Tuesday — better get my tennis shoes ready."

Step Five—Decide how you'll reward yourself when you've reached your goal. Will you use your saved-up allowance to get a new CD to dance to? Read your favorite book all the way through again? Make yourself a killer smoothie? God smiles on you when you make an effort to take care of the body he's given you, so make plans to smile on yourself with a treat.

Step Six—Once you've reached your goal and rewarded yourself, set a new goal and a new reward. After all, we're never finished exercising. You're starting a lifelong habit.

IT: As part of your decision to get your body moving and healthy, take a look at how much time you spend doing nonactive things. That would include playing video games, sitting in front of the computer, watching TV or movies, and reading. There is nothing wrong with any of those activities, but if you're spending more than two hours a day at any one of them, you're cutting into moving-around time. You already sit for a lot of your time at school, not to mention while you're riding in the car, eating, and doing homework. If you spend much more time on your buns, you run the risk of being <u>sedentary</u>, which means you're not burning enough calories to keep your body running in good condition. Try curling up with your book <u>after</u> you walk the dog, or catching your fave TV show while you're resting up from a wild game of hide-and-seek.

Just as important as exercise is its opposite—sleep. Whether you snooze like a kitten or would love to stay up all night, these guidelines are for you and all girls your age:

Get enough sleep so that when you get up in the morning, you are wide awake and alert within fifteen to thirty minutes (even if you aren't a "morning person").

Be sure "enough sleep" is at least eight hours a night.

Always go to bed and get up at the same times, except on weekends and holidays. (Even then, don't get off your routine too much.)

Sleep in loose, soft clothing. Be sure you won't be too hot.

Have a regular, unwinding routine that you follow before bed so you can fall asleep within a half hour. Maybe it's a hot bath, a protein snack like turkey, and night-time prayers. Some girls like to write in a journal to sort out all the stuff of the day. Others let music calm them down. Going to sleep with the TV on isn't the best choice.

You'll sleep best if your room doesn't look like an earthquake hit. Tidy up some before you crawl under the covers.

Within two hours of bedtime, don't drink caffeine, eat a big meal, or watch scary or upsetting TV or movies. Do exercise during the day, but not right before you go to bed.

If you lie awake for longer than a half hour every night or have major nightmares, talk to your mom or dad about it. You may have things bothering you that even you aren't aware of.

You're Good to Go

So how cool would it be to have your own personal fitness plan that you could consult often? Serious athletes keep a log of their activities — often in a small book. You can put one together, especially designed for the unique You. If you want, get your Sisterhood together so you can each make one.

What you'll need:

the fitness plan information and choices you gathered in Steps One through Six under "Here's the Deal" on pages 62–64

a blank book or small binder filled with paper, purchased or homemade (with heavier paper or cardboard for the cover and blank white pages stapled inside)

a cool pen or marker

pictures of your favorite sports or activities from magazines or your own photo collection

glue stick

What to do:

Decorate your blank book however you want with pictures and quotes to inspire you.

Set up a page for each week. Put your goal at the top and divide the page into three columns. List down the left side the days and times you're going to work toward your goal. In the center column, write what you actually do, for how long, how many times, and those kinds of things. On the right, you can make notes, such as, "This is getting easier," "Coach said I was improving," and "I think my tennis shoes are too small."

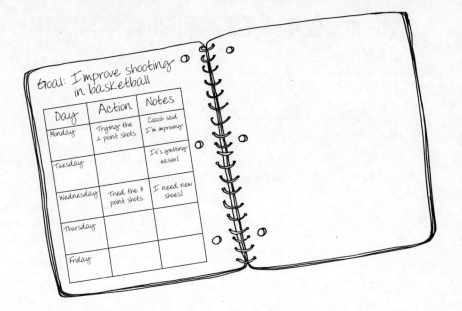

Goal: Improve shooting in basketball

Day	Action	Notes
Monday	Trying the 2 point shots	Coach said I'm improving
Tuesday		It's getting easier!
Wednesday	Tried the 3 point shots	I need new shoes!
Thursday		
Friday		

You can design one section of the book for listing ways you'd like to reward yourself, so when you meet your goal, you can choose one. That's a fun section for "dream pictures."

What it tells you:

That you're actually doing what you set out to do.

That a little bit at a time can make a real difference in how you feel.

What to do now:

Keep your fitness plan book in your gym bag with your other equipment and fill it in after every practice, game, or play session.

When you reach your goal, set up a new one (with new rewards!). When you can actually see yourself making progress, you'll want to make even more.

That's What I'm Talkin' About!

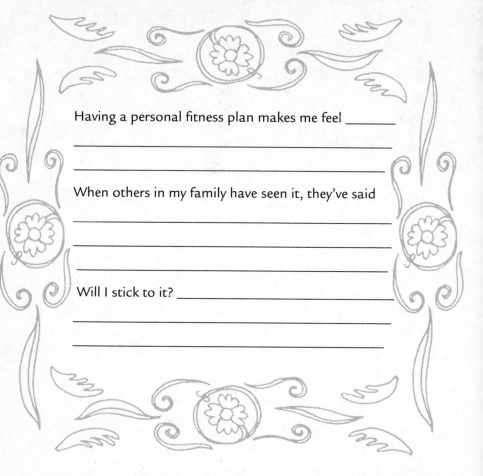

Having a personal fitness plan makes me feel _____

_____

_____

When others in my family have seen it, they've said

_____

_____

_____

Will I stick to it? _____

_____

_____

chapter five

Table
TALK

I'm hungry," Courtney announced. She opened the pantry and stared at the contents.

"You're hungry again?" her dad said. He joined her, looking at his watch. "You just ate."

"Da-ad," she said. "That was *before* I rode my bike for, like, an hour."

He tugged at her ponytail. "I forget you aren't a couch potato anymore. So, what's it gonna be?" He pointed to a bag of chips. "Doritos? Cookies? PB&J?"

Courtney reached for a box of cereal — the kind with the colored marshmallows — opened it, and stuck her hand inside.

"You don't want a bowl?" Dad said.

She shook her head. "I like them dry. Don't worry — I won't eat the whole box."

Dad pulled out the chips and a jar of salsa. "See you in an hour," he said.

"What happens in an hour?"

He grinned. "That's when you'll be hungry again."

Fathers think they're so clever. Courtney took her snack to the family room and turned on the TV. But halfway through *Hannah Montana* — and the cereal — she felt tired and curled into a ball on the couch. It was weird. She was kind of jittery, but she didn't have the energy to even grab the box from her little brother when he passed through and snatched it.

Huh. She thought exercise was supposed to make her more energetic. Right now, she felt like a blob.

"Courtney!" her mom called from the kitchen. "Dinner's ready!"

All Courtney could say was, "Ug."

That Is SO Me!

Before we talk about what Courtney — and you — need to eat (and not eat) to avoid blob-itis, let's see what you're putting into your body these days. Have fun with this quiz. It isn't here to make you feel guilty, but to get you on the way to being as healthy as you can be.

Under each menu below, circle the number that's closest to what you eat most often for that meal. (Not the one you think you should eat, but the one that actually goes into your body.)

Breakfast Menu

1. donut, muffin, or microwave/toaster treat
2. cold cereal, toast, or waffles/pancakes
3. fruit, yogurt, or a smoothie
4. eggs, smoothie with protein powder, or hot cereal

Morning Snack Menu

1. donut, muffin, or candy bar
2. granola bar, crackers and cheese, or fruit juice
3. fresh fruit, yogurt, or raisins
4. celery with peanut butter, trail mix, or milk

Lunch Menu

1. pizza, chicken nuggets, or burger and fries
2. lunch meat, cheese, or PB&J on white or plain wheat bread
3. tuna, chicken, or turkey sandwich on whole-grain bread
4. veggie soup, tuna or chicken on salad, or turkey wrap with lettuce and tomatoes

Afternoon Snack Menu

1. cookies, chips, or microwaved snack like Hot Pockets
2. popcorn, pretzels, or milk shake

3   peanut butter and whole-wheat crackers, a fruit smoothie, or a bowl of non-sugary cereal

4   raw veggies, fresh fruit, or no-sugar-added yogurt

Dinner Menu

1   frozen dinner, pizza, or supper at a fast-food restaurant

2   fried chicken and mashed potatoes, SpaghettiOs and apple-sauce, or macaroni and cheese

3   steak, baked potato, and salad or barbecue chicken, rice, and peas

4   baked chicken, broccoli, and green salad or broiled fish, string beans, and fruit salad

Bedtime Snack Menu

1   cookies and milk, cereal with sugar and milk, or a pudding cup

2   popcorn, fruit juice, or chocolate milk

3   peanut butter and crackers, cheese, or plain milk

4   turkey slice, non-caffeinated tea with milk, warm milk

Add together the numbers you've circled. You'll come up with a total between six and twenty-four, which you can write here: _____

Let's see what that might say about your "fuel supply."

If your total was between 6 and 9, your diet has some pretty big nutrition holes in it. You're probably not getting very many of the things you need to be strong and healthy and to grow as much as you need to. You may even get sick often. That can be fixed. We'll show you how to fix that. For now, do *not* go to your mom and tell her she's not feeding you right!

If your total is between 10 and 14, you're getting some of the things from food that you need for health and growth, but you would feel better and have more energy if you ate more nutritious foods. That can be fixed. Meanwhile, don't complain about your diet to your mom! This chapter is about *your* choices.

continued on next page...

If your total is between 15 and 19, you have a pretty healthy diet, and it probably shows in how you feel and how much energy you have. Even if you didn't change a thing, you'd be healthy and strong. This chapter will just help you see any gaps you might have in your diet that could be filled with some yummy things.

If your total is between 20 and 24, you're very unusual for your age! You have an excellent chance of being in amazing physical shape. It's okay, by the way, to treat yourself to a little fun "kid food" once in a while. Read on for some safe ways to do that.

Here's the Deal

Remember that we said you're growing more in your tween years than in any other period of your life? Between that and the exercise you're getting (You *are*, aren't you?), you obviously need the right fuel. Not just anything you can get your hands on, but the real stuff your body needs for all the growing and changing it's doing.

You've probably already figured out that the box of sugary cereal wasn't Courtney's best choice for an after-bike-riding snack. It wasn't the exercise that made her feel like one of the cushions on the couch; it was the wrong fuel going in to replace what she'd burned off . . . not to mention the fact that she didn't get herself a glass of water first.

So what should Courtney—and you—eat to keep your bodies going strong?

What You Need to Eat Every Day

This is the Pyramid Plan designed by the USDA, the US Department of Agriculture. It shows the proportions you should eat from each food group. The columns are wider on the bottom to remind you to eat more of the leaner choices from each category.

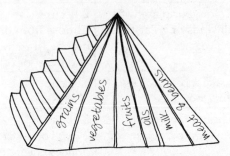

make half your grains whole

get your calcium-rich foods

vary your veggies

focus on fruits

know your fats

go lean on protein

My Pyramid Guidelines

Grains	Make at least half your grains whole grains.	6 ounces One-ounce equivalents: one slice of bread; one cup dry cereal; ½ cup cooked rice, pasta, or cereal
Vegetables	Color your plate with all kinds of great-tasting veggies.	2 ½ cups Choose from dark green, orange, starchy, dry beans and peas, or other veggies
Fruits	Make most choices fruit, not juice	1 ½ cups
Milk	Choose fat-free or lowfat most often.	3 cups 1 cup yogurt or 1 ½ ounces cheese equals one cup milk
Meat and Beans	Choose lean meat and chicken or turkey. Vary your choices — more fish, beans, peas, nuts, and seeds.	5 ounces One-ounce equivalents: one ounce meat, chicken, turkey, or fish; one egg; one tablespoon peanut butter; ½ ounce nuts; or ¼ cup dry beans
Physical Activity	Build more physical activity into your daily routine at home and school.	At least 60 minutes of moderate to vigorous activity a day or most days.

These quantities are designed for a girl of ten who does thirty to sixty minutes of physical activity a day (the steps on the pyramid are a reminder of the importance of exercise). If you want to have a more personalized plan, go to *www.MyPyramid.gov* and the website will show you how.

You may be asking, "Uh, where do my sodas and candy bars and salad dressing and stuff go on the pyramid?" They actually don't fit into any group. They're extras which are mainly fat and sugar, and you should use them "sparingly." *Sparingly* means "once in a while." Here are some guidelines:

- You should consume *no more than sixty grams of fat* a day. A Double Whopper with cheese and mayo has 69 grams of fat. If you become a label reader, you'll discover how fast those fats can add up.
- You should consume *no more than ten teaspoons of sugar a day.* That may sound like a lot, but it adds up quickly. With your mom's permission, measure 18 teaspoons of sugar into a glass of water. Would you drink that? Yuck! But that's how much sugar is in a 20-ounce bottle of soda. A Cinnabon has 11 teaspoons of sugar. A 12-ounce McFlurry with M&Ms has 18 teaspoons of sugar. Check the labels of things like salad dressing, spaghetti sauce, and soup, and try not to eat anything with more than 4 grams of sugar (5 grams equals about one teaspoon).

IT: While you're chowing down on good food, remember to drink water. Your body is ninety percent water, so you need lots — like eight glasses a day. Soda, juice, and milk don't count — it has to be plain old H_2O. A lot of girls say they don't like water, but that's probably because they're used to trying to quench their thirst with other things that, quite frankly, taste better. But once you develop the water habit, you'll learn to love it, really. Nothing takes away thirst better, and it gives you so much energy. In fact, next time you're really hungry and it isn't mealtime, drink a big glass of water and see if that helps. Sometimes when you think you're hungry, your body is really telling you it's thirsty.

What You Need to Eat When

Certain foods will fuel you better if you eat them at the right times. Try these "timed treats"—and you will *rock*!

For all-day energy

* Start off with a healthy breakfast, even if it isn't breakfast food.
* Eat a healthy snack at midmorning and in the mid-afternoon. Three meals are not enough to get you through the day. You need body and brain food every few hours.

For a big-test day (especially those standardized tests that come every couple of years and last all day)

* Eat an especially good breakfast.
* Avoid sugary snacks which will make you sleepy once the big energy spike is gone.

Before really strenuous physical activity (like a game or a big practice or a family hike)

* Eat complex carbohydrates like fruit, whole-grain bread, or raw veggies, which will burn while you're active and keep giving you energy.
* Eating a sweet snack will give you a burst of energy, but it won't last long, and when it's gone, you'll *crash*!

To help you fall asleep quickly and easily at night

* Do *not* eat foods containing sugar or anything really fatty or greasy within two hours of going to bed.
* Do *not* drink any caffeine within six hours of going to bed. That means no cola after midafternoon.
* *Do* eat turkey before you go to bed if you have trouble falling asleep. It has *tryptophan* in it which promotes sleepiness if you eat it with an empty tummy.
* Milk is good before bed too, especially if it's warmed up.
* The later dinner is, the lighter it should be. If you're having a late supper, eat veggies, whole grains, and

lean protein like turkey or chicken, rather than a big ol' steak with a baked potato and sour cream or a huge plate of spaghetti.

What Not to Eat — EVER! (If you can help it)

Your pencil eraser.

No, seriously, there are some foods that just don't help your body and can actually hurt it. Once in a while, okay, but you can enjoy substitutes that actually *do* something for you. BTW, foods that give you absolutely nothing are called *empty calories*.

Instead of These Unhealthy Choices:	Enjoy These Alternatives:
soda	milk fruit juice (½ cup a day) water
artificial sweeteners	small amount of honey a little bit of brown sugar cinnamon
any foods with sugar as the first ingredient listed on a package	fruit raisins fruit spread on bread
crackers and chips containing partially hydrogenated oil	pretzels whole-grain crackers high-fiber graham crackers rice cakes
margarine	Smart Balance butter
snacks and cereals made with corn	cereals made with whole wheat or rice
store-bought cookies	homemade cookies baked with whole-wheat flour, brown sugar, and other healthy ingredients

What about Fast Food?

It's so fun to go to McDonald's with the team after a big victory, or have breakfast at Burger King with your dad on Saturday morning before you hit Toys "R" Us. Go! Enjoy! Just don't do it every day or even every week if you can help it. Here's why:

- It's super processed, which means it's loaded with chemicals that are hard on your liver, your heart, and your stomach.
- It's high in fat, which is hard to digest and adds calories that stay on you instead of burning off; the fried stuff is the worst.
- The bread (usually) isn't whole grain, so it has more sugar and doesn't have the fiber you need for your digestion.
- The portions are way too big; one Double Whopper with cheese and mayo has 1,060 calories—and you only need a total of 1,800 in a whole day!
- Some "meals" automatically come with a soda, which is loaded with salt and sugar; its carbonation has acid which isn't good for your tummy, teeth, or bones.

When you do go out for fast food on a fun occasion, the following menu items are your best choices because they have the least amount of calories, salt, chemicals, and unhealthy fat:

- KFC—Original Recipe Chicken Breast without skin or breading
- Burger King—Chicken Whopper (without mayo), or BK Veggie Burger
- McDonald's—Hamburger
- Subway—Veggie Delite 6-inch sub
- Taco Bell—Fresco Style Crunchy Taco
- Wendy's—Jr. Hamburger

Forget the fries and go for the fruit some fast-food places now offer. Choose milk or orange juice instead of soda, and you're good to go.

Here's the Deal

You might be really jazzed about eating a healthier diet, but you might also be thinking, "Hello-o! I don't do the grocery shopping. I don't decide what we have for dinner."

Well, there is that, isn't there? A lot of families are so busy with sports practices and after-school lessons and church activities, dinner is often served from a drive-through window and eaten in the backseat of the car. Even if you do eat at home, meals might be popped out of a box because there's so much going on.

But did you know that young people your age influence (on the average) one out of every three spending decisions a family makes? Usually that means kids are whining for Game Boys, iPods, and cell phones—but why not put in your vote for healthier food? (And remember, do *not* tell your parents they've been feeding you all wrong and you are now going to set them straight; they won't appreciate it!) Here are some ways you can take charge of your food choices:

* Volunteer to go grocery shopping with whoever does that chore in your family. And instead of begging for the cereal with the marshmallows, ask for a whole-grain choice that doesn't have more than four grams of sugar per serving. See if your mom or dad will buy grapes instead of cookies, whole-wheat bread instead of white, and pretzels instead of chips. They may want to know who you are and what you've done with their daughter, but when they recover they'll probably be proud of you.

Ask if you can help plan meals for the week. Make a cool menu sheet by hand or on the computer to post on the refrigerator. Ask family members what they want for suppers and use this book to make their selections as healthy as possible.

Hang out in the kitchen and help with the cooking. If your parents don't have time to chop up stuff for a salad, you can totally do that. If it's too hectic in the afternoon to make smoothies before soccer practice, step up to the plate (or blender) yourself and do it.

Pack your own nutritious lunch, since school lunch isn't always the healthiest meal on the planet. Include baby carrots and grapes instead of chips and cookies. Make a killer sandwich that will have everybody at the table drooling. Pop in the occasional treat — like homemade cookies — maybe on Fridays.

When Mom and Dad want to know where you'd like to eat out, don't automatically shout for your favorite pizza place, or if you do, get a salad and eat it before you dig into a double cheese with pepperoni.

When you're hanging out with your friends, grab a juice or water instead of a soda. Eat one handful of chips instead of half the bag. Better yet, carry raisins, healthy crackers, or a small bag of trail mix in your backpack.

If anybody teases you about your healthy eating habits, that's one of the few times it's appropriate to roll your eyes (unless it's at your mom or dad; you have to put up with them!). Why let some unhealthy person tell you how to eat? You have the power to feed yourself the right way, so smile and chomp away on that celery stick with natural peanut butter. Then knock their socks off on the soccer field, in the spelling bee, or at the next sleepover laugh fest, because you can do that when you fuel your body with the best stuff possible.

It totally doesn't take a rocket scientist to figure out that God is behind this whole feed-your-body-right thing. There are hundreds of verses about food in the Bible! Here are just a few of the things God says about how we should eat.

God said, "I give you every seed-bearing plant on the face of the whole earth and every tree that has fruit with seed in it. They will be yours for food." — GENESIS 1:29

Sure sounds like fruits and veggies and grains. You don't hear anything about Twinkies and Pop-Tarts in there, do you?

"Of all the animals that live on land, these are the ones you may eat." — LEVITICUS 11:2

BTW: Sugar comes from sugar cane, which you can chew on to your heart's content. It's the refining of it that makes it hard for your body to use. The same goes for white flour. We need to keep fruits, veggies, and grains as close to their natural state as we can.

God goes on to give forty-six verses worth of instructions about what animals to eat and how to cook them. Does it sound to you like God cares about the meat we put into our bodies? The point is not that we follow all of that exactly (although how hard would it be not to eat camel, rabbit, or vulture meat?), but that we pay attention to how natural and well-cooked our meat is. It's safe to say God did not envision a flat burger that's made mostly of icky fillers that clog up your body.

When you sit to dine with a ruler,
note well what is before you,
and put a knife to your throat
if you are given to gluttony.
Do not crave his delicacies,
for that food is deceptive.
— PROVERBS 23:1-3

Before you freak out, this doesn't mean you should literally take a blade to your neck! The verses tell you several things:

Don't think stuffing yourself with sweet, gooey, creamy treats is going to make you happy or accepted.

If you catch yourself eating junk when you're nervous or upset or unhappy, stop! Cut off that habit (not your throat), and do something healthy for yourself—talk to someone about what's bothering you, get some exercise to clear your head, or write to God about your troubles in a journal.

If overeating and weighing so much that you can't enjoy physical activities or fun clothes is part of your life, ask a grown-up to help you. It isn't about how you look (and fitting in with the popular kids at school); it's about how you feel in mind and body.

> When you have eaten and are satisfied,
> praise the Lord your God for the good land
> he has given you. — DEUTERONOMY 8:10

God is warning us here not to take all the credit for the good things that happen to us. But this verse is also a reminder to be grateful for all the wonderful food choices we have and to eat and be satisfied. That means, don't let yourself get hungry because you think you'll get fat if you eat. Don't skip breakfast or lunch because you want to be skinny like the models in the magazines. Don't go on a weight-loss diet unless a *doctor* says you need to for health reasons—and even then, eat healthy food and get exercise instead of starving yourself.

You are not too young to be in danger of developing an *eating disorder*, such as *anorexia*, where a person deprives herself of food to the point of illness, or *bulimia*, where she stuffs in as much food as she can and then throws it up. If you are tempted to do either of these, go to an adult you trust immediately. An eating disorder is a sickness that can follow you your whole life if it isn't treated right away. You are a growing young woman. Eat and be satisfied!

You're Good to Go

Now would be a good time to try out some of the things you've read about in this chapter. You may be ready to go all out, so all of the new activities are combined in this section, "Food Fun for a Physically Fit Me." But if you only have a little bit of time or you want to start small, choose any part below that sounds fun to you and just do that. Let it be something you enjoy. After a couple of weeks, review your progress and your feelings about your choices (see "That's What I'm Talkin' About!" on page 86).

Food Fun for a Physically Fit Me

Part 1: Create a worksheet to record your food and exercise for a week. Refer to the suggestions on the food pyramid. Figure out what you're actually eating and how you could improve that. See sample worksheet below.

Meals	Day One	Day Two	Day Three	Day Four
Breakfast				
Midmorning Snack				
Lunch				
Midafternoon Snack				
Dinner				
Bedtime Snack				
Exercise				

Part 2: Ask the family cook (Mom or Dad) if you could help plan menus for a week. Use this book to make suggestions for meals that fit the pyramid guidelines.

Part 3: Be a grocery-shopping assistant. Volunteer to go to the food store with the family shopper and, using this book, suggest healthy choices. If the shopper doesn't want to buy what you suggest for the whole family, ask if you can have a small snack drawer or basket of your own.

Part 4: Become the chef's apprentice. Ask if you can help in the kitchen — chopping veggies, cutting up fruit, learning how to steam vegetables, and making salads. Eating healthy is more work, so if you're going to suggest that meals be healthier, you'll need to be willing to do some of the tasks involved.

Part 5: Have fun helping the cook make things look wonderful before you put them on the table. Could you include a sprig of parsley on each plate? Arrange the cherry tomatoes in a design on top of the salad? Pour the milk in pretty glasses and fold the napkins?

What you'll need:

- this book
- a menu-planning sheet you make yourself
- a pad of paper for a grocery list
- clean hands and a willingness to learn

What to do:

- Always ask if you can help. Barging right in and saying, "Okay, I'm going to show you people how this is done" never really works.
- Explain that you know how hard it is to feed a family a healthy diet and that you just want to help by sharing what you're learning.
- Be sure you can commit on a regular basis to whatever you volunteer to do. Going to the store and talking Mom into buying fresh veggies and then disappearing when it's time to wash and chop them isn't going to win you any friends in the kitchen!

What it tells you:

- That you really are serious about taking care of your temple/body.
- That you're showing grown-up responsibility.

What to do now:

Enjoy!

That's What I'm Talkin' About!

After two weeks of "Food Fun for a Physically Fit Me," this is how I feel:

In body: _____

_____

_____

In mind: _____

_____

In emotions: _____

_____

In the joy factor: _____

_____

chapter six

The Clean
SCENE

"Courtney stinks."

Courtney wrinkled her nose at her little brother Sam. "You don't exactly smell like a perfume counter yourself."

Her other little brother, Will, sniffed the air. "Sam just smells like those chips we ate. *You* smell like BO."

"Mo-om!"

"You boys leave your sister alone," Courtney's mom said as she shooed the boys out of the kitchen. "Go insult each other someplace else."

They held their noses as they passed Courtney on the way out the door.

"Do I really stink?" Courtney said when they were gone.

"You've smelled better," Mom said. "But what do you expect when you just finished a two-hour soccer practice and you haven't showered yet?" She reached into the grocery bag she was unpacking and tossed something to Courtney. "As a matter of fact, I just bought you something."

"What is it?" Courtney said. She caught the blue plastic container. "Deodorant?"

"Your very own. Put it on after you shower."

"Then I *do* stink!" Courtney wailed.

"It comes with growing up, honey. It's nothing a little personal hygiene won't take care of. Oh, and Court?" Mom nodded at Courtney's feet. "Leave those tennis shoes in the mudroom, would you?"

"Why?" Courtney said. But then she held up her hand. "I know — they smell too."

Whew. This growing-up business really stunk.

Here's the Deal

 Remember those hormones we talked about in chapter one? The ones that bring on puberty? They not only change the way your body looks and functions, but they change the way it smells. Lovely, huh? These are the odor issues you'll want to pay attention to:

- general body odor (what Courtney's little brothers referred to as BO)
- underarm odor (body odor's favorite breeding place)
- stinky feet (with a lovely aroma all their own)

Why now, when you already have bras and periods and hairy legs to think about? Because those same hormones increase the amount of sweat your sweat glands produce, and — with millions of those little glands in your body — that can be a lot of perspiration when you're hot, active, or nervous. Sweat is actually a good thing, because when it evaporates, your skin cools down, and it removes toxins (icky stuff) from your body.

Good or not, sweat can create a smelly situation. Special sweat glands in your underarms and between your legs become active for the first time during puberty (those hormones again). It isn't the sweat itself that causes that less than delicious aroma; it's the bacteria living on your skin that breaks down the sweat and causes an odor. Those little critters really like the sweat in your armpits and genital (between your legs) area. Besides, it's warm and dark in those places, perfect conditions for bacteria to make more bacteria.

So what do you do about it? This is one of the easiest parts of puberty. Just take these simple steps:

- Ignore commercials and magazine ads that say pit odor will ruin your life! If somebody doesn't want to be your friend because you're a little stinky between horseback riding and the shower, she needs to take a whiff of her own self! *Everybody* perspires.
- Take a bath or shower every day (and maybe every other day in winter) to wash off bacteria. Pay special attention to those breeding areas. If you've taken a shower in the morning and you get sweaty during the day, at least wash your pits before you hang out with people again.
- Wear clean clothes. Bacteria hang out on fabric that hasn't made it to the laundry.
- If you tend to sweat a lot, wear clothes that "breathe," like 100% cotton. It absorbs more moisture and lets air circulate, which helps keep you dry.
- If you don't like the way your armpits smell, use a *deodorant,* which covers up the body odor with a nice scent of its own, or an *antiperspirant*, which cuts down on the amount of sweat you produce.
  - ✳ No one is quite sure whether the aluminum in these products is safe for you, so if you want to be extra careful, choose a deodorant without aluminum or an antiperspirant with "buffered aluminum sulfate."
  - ✳ Always follow the directions on the label.
  - ✳ Be sure, of course, to wash under your arms before you apply deodorant or antiperspirant.
- If your genital area has an unfamiliar odor, *do not use a feminine hygiene spray*. It can cause irritation. If you wash every day and wear clean cotton underwear, that area shouldn't smell. If it does, you might have an infection, so talk to your mom.

IT: If your armpits turn dark gray or black (and it's your skin, not hair, that's darkening your underarms), you might have a buildup of dry skin from antiperspirants and shaving. Try a lotion that has lactic acid for six weeks. If that doesn't help, your dark armpits could be genetic (which means the pigmentation runs in the family), or you could have high insulin levels (especially if you're also dark around your neck, waistline, knuckles, or elbows). A doctor can give you a bleaching cream or check your insulin levels. If you're self-conscious, don't go sleeveless until you get it cleared up — but remember that it's nothing to be ashamed of.

Stinky feet create a special brand of yuckiness, especially if you spend most of your day in tennis shoes and socks. If you gag when you kick off your tennies, here are some simple remedies:

Be sure your feet are clean before you put on your socks and shoes.

Sprinkle baby powder, talcum powder, or special foot powder inside your shoes or socks.

Wear clean cotton or wool socks. Natural fibers will absorb the sweat instead of leaving it on your feet.

Wear shoes made of natural materials like leather or canvas, which will let your feet breathe. Try to avoid plastic in your footwear.

If your current shoes are giving off a smell, sprinkle baking soda in them at night and then shake them out in the morning. If that doesn't do the job, try a special product like Odor Eaters. Still no luck? Buy new shoes!

Wear shoes other than tennies when you can.

Don't stress out if your feet are a little smelly; human beings are, after all, supposed to smell like people!

Finally, there's your breath. There was nothing sweeter than that sweet baby-girlfriend breath you used to have, even when you first woke up. Now, well, not so much. No worries, though. Just add these steps to your "Clean Routine."

- Brush your teeth twice a day — in the morning and at night. It doesn't hurt to give them a touch-up if you're sprucing up to go out to supper or to a friend's for a birthday party.

- Floss your teeth at least once a day. Yeah, it takes time you'd rather be using for something else, so do it while you're reading a book or watching TV. It cuts down on plaque, which gathers up bacteria on your teeth (and you already know the stink bacteria can raise).

- Rinse with mouthwash after you brush to kill the germs you don't need; again, they're the culprits who cause icky odors.

- Strong-smelling foods like onions and garlic stay on your breath. If you can't brush your teeth after that Italian dinner or burger with the big ol' onion slice, rinse with water, eat an apple, or suck on a breath mint. If you can't do any of those, don't worry about it. Again, bad breath is not death to your social life — no matter what the commercials might tell you.

- If you still have breath issues after all of that (and most people don't), ask your dentist about it next time you visit (which you should do every six months). The doc can tell if you need a prescription mouthwash or if you might have something else going on in your body (which is very rare, so don't freak out!).

IT: *Although they don't fall into the could-smell-bad category, nails, hair, and skin need more care now that you're on your way to womanhood. To find out how to keep those parts of you clean, see another Faithgirlz book called Beauty Lab — and enjoy!*

GOT GOD?

So if God made our bodies full of sweat glands and hormones and pits and cavities for bacteria to set up housekeeping in, why do we have to worry about being odor-free?

God doesn't tell us to *worry* about it. Advertisers, who want to sell soap, deodorant, foot spray, and mouthwash tell us we need to get rid of every human smell so we'll be liked by everyone. They're the ones who want us to stress out. God just wants us to be clean.

In the book of Leviticus, which was the handbook of rules for the Israelites when they were traveling through the wilderness to the Promised Land, there are six chapters about "the clean" and "the unclean." Chapter 11 talks about food. Chapter 12 tells women how to be purified after they have a baby. In chapters 13 and 14, you can find out everything you ever wanted to know about skin diseases and mildew. Need to find out about unclean "discharges"? The answers are in chapter 15.

God provided all of that for two reasons. First, he wanted his people to live long and healthy lives. Naturally, then, he taught them about rotten food and other things that would make them sick. And secondly, he wanted them to think about him in absolutely everything they did — even in the way they washed their hands and tidied their tents.

God still wants the same thing for us. He wants us disease-free, without a bunch of bacteria taking over our bodies. If we're sick, we can't do what he's put us here to do. And God still wants us to live lives that are all about him and his love. One of the loveliest ways to do that is to cleanse our bodies and present our best selves before him, just as the Israelites did.

While we're thinking about being clean on the outside, God hopes we'll think a *lot* about cleaning up our act on the inside. In fact, God reminds us throughout the Bible, with verses like this:

He [or she] who has clean hands and a pure heart...will receive blessing from the Lord.
— PSALM 24:4-5

Those "clean hands" stand for the good things we do with our hands (our actions), and the "pure heart" is the love inside that makes us want to do those good things in the first place. So just being scrubbed of every speck of dirt and deodorized from every smell isn't all that God wants. It's the cleanness of our very selves — what we believe and what we do — that really counts.

So while you're taking a shower or sprinkling baking soda in your tennis shoes, look inside yourself too, and bathe away that desire to flush your little brother down the toilet, and scrub out the need to be more popular than Miss Thing over there. When your true self is shining, who cares about a little soccer sweat?

That Is SO Me!

Don't worry. We're not going to ask you to choose teams and sniff at each other like puppies! Just think about each of these basic hygiene habits and put a check next to the ones you're already doing. (And, no, you are not a pig if you end up with very few check marks!)

_____ I take a bath or shower every day.

_____ I actually use soap when I take a bath or shower!

_____ I wear clean clothes every day.

_____ I brush my teeth twice a day.

_____ I floss my teeth once a day.

_____ I rinse with mouthwash at least once a day.

_____ I now use a deodorant or antiperspirant because I've noticed my underarms have a smell.

_____ I wear cotton or wool socks.

_____ I wear cotton underwear.

_____ I treat my tennis shoes when they smell.

_____ I talk to my mom or another adult I trust when I have odors which bother me that I can't get rid of.

_____ I'm kind about other people's odor issues; I don't point them out in public, tease, or act disgusted.

_____ I just let it go if I'm smelly and can't do anything about it right then.

_____ I pay as much attention to keeping my inside self clean as I do my outside self.

Now just look back at the items you _didn't_ check. Can you do something to get those taken care of if they apply to you? (You might not be ready for deodorant yet or have any problems with odiferous feet.) Our next section is designed to help you, so let's go for it.

The best way to develop a new habit is to start with one small thing.

One Small Thing

Choose one item under "That Is SO Me!" that you did NOT check off and write it here. _____

_____

What you'll need:

Make a list of supplies for whatever new thing you're adding to your Clean Routine.

EXAMPLE: For dealing with underarm odor, I'll need

- soap or body wash
- washcloth or loofah
- a deodorant I like the smell of (without aluminum)

What to do:

Make a written reminder for yourself and put it where you'll see it at the right time. You can write on an index card, put up a sticky note, or create something fun on your computer. A reminder to use mouthwash could go inside the medicine cabinet. Put a note to sprinkle baby powder in your socks in your sock drawer. Be creative, and have fun with it.

What it tells you:

That you're becoming a responsible young woman who doesn't sit around and whine about how much trouble it is to grow up, but instead takes on her new tasks like the mature person she is. It also tells you that you're ready for some of the good parts of growing up, like having more choices. It's all going to be worth it.

What to do now:

A new task usually becomes a habit after two weeks. Then you can work on another item from the list. One step at a time — that's how we make our lives better.

That's What I'm Talkin' About!

Now that you're one step closer to a cleaner, healthier you, how do you feel about your sweet self?

Somebody noticed a change in me: _____

_____

_____

I feel more _____

_____

_____

It's not so bad because _____

_____

_____

chapter seven

That Whole
BOY THING

He is SO cute!" Sydney said.

"Cute? He's a total hottie," Anna said.

Courtney got ready to roll her eyes. They were always talking about boys now: how this one looked at them and that one actually smiled at them. What was the big deal?

"Psst! Court!" Sydney hissed. "He's looking at *you*!"

Anna took Courtney by the shoulders and turned her around. A sixth-grade boy stared over the top of the book he had in front of him. He ducked behind it the same minute Courtney realized he really was looking at her.

Yesterday, she might have said, "Hey, why don't you take a picture? It would last longer." Or she would have prepared herself for the rude remark that was sure to come out of him because he was a boy. Or she might have wondered where the rest of his cootie-infested pack was with their spitballs and water balloons.

But today, something else happened. Courtney felt her face getting warm, slowly, from her neck up to the roots of her hair. Her heart acted strangely, like it couldn't find the right beat. And her mind clearly said, "He was looking at me? Like, *really* looking?"

Beside her, Sydney giggled. "You like him, don't you," she whispered.

"I don't even *know* him!"

"Who said you had to know him?" Anna whispered on her other side. "All you have to do is look at him to have a crush on him."

"I don't have a crush on him," Courtney muttered behind her hand.

"SHHHHHH!" the librarian sprayed from behind her counter.

Courtney could have hugged her. At least now she could hide in the shelves and try to figure out just what was going on. How could she, Courtney the Cootie Counter, suddenly feel all fluttery because a boy — okay, a cute boy — looked at her like she was a girl?

There must be some other explanation. Maybe she was coming down with the flu. Or it could have been the school lunch. Still, just before she skittered down the biography aisle, she took one last glance at Cute Boy.

His eyes were twinkling at her over the top of his book.

GOT GOD?

We definitely need to go straight to God with this one! Yes, noticing boys in a different way than you used to is part of puberty too. And you can blame those hormones — or thank them!

The same hormones that God puts into action so you can have babies cause you to be attracted to guys so you'll *want* to have their kids. Of course, that wasn't such a big deal back in biblical times (and even up until about a hundred years ago), when girls didn't reach puberty until they were fourteen and then got married not long after. In today's world, you're more likely to start puberty at age ten and not get married until you're in your twenties. That's more than a decade!

That's why it's really important to know what God wants when it comes to you and boys. Otherwise, all those feelings that come with liking a boy's attention can get pretty confusing. There are things from the Bible we know for sure.

> A man will leave his father and mother and be united to his wife, and they will become one flesh.
> — GENESIS 2:24

God set it up from the very beginning that men and women are supposed to be partners and become like one person, not just in body, but in building a life together. He definitely made it so men and women would be attracted to each other. As we've mentioned before, the minute Adam laid eyes on Eve, he said, "This is now bone of my bones and flesh of my flesh" (Genesis 2:23). Which means, "She is human, made by God, as I am."

Then God set up a simple guideline to protect a couple when they decide to spend their lives together. "You shall not commit adultery" (Exodus 20:14). It's one of the Ten Commandments, the rules for living, and it means, "Don't do married-people stuff with somebody you're not married to." If your parents haven't already talked to you about the special, physical things a husband and wife do together, which can be the start of a baby, it's up to you whether you want to ask them about that. It will be a special conversation that will explain a lot about the purpose of puberty. For now, just know that God makes it clear and simple: save those special things for marriage.

After puberty takes hold, your body and mind will want to take you close to the cute boy who makes you feel special. There is nothing wrong with the desire itself; that's how God made you. The challenge is not to let it tell you what you're going to do. Whole books have been written about purity — which is what we're talking about here — and you'll probably read some of them as you get older. You'll definitely hear a lot about it when you're a teenager. Right now, though, is a good time to fill your mind and heart with something that will make the challenge easier for you as boys grow cuter to you and become less like absurd little creeps. That something is God's "whatever."

> Whatever is true, whatever is noble, whatever is right, whatever is pure, whatever is lovely, whatever is admirable — if anything is excellent or praiseworthy — think about such things. Whatever you have learned or received or heard from me, or seen in me — put it into practice. And the God of peace will be with you.
> — PHILIPPIANS 4:8-9

Here's the Deal

So do you hide someplace like Courtney did until you're ready to get married? That would be a long time spent in the library shelves! These years are the time to get to know what boys are like (because they are *so* different from girls — or haven't you noticed?). Let's take a look at some of the boy-girl relationships you might experience before your teen years:

Having boys as friends — Boys can make really good pals because they don't tend to gossip and get jealous of your other friends — you know, the kind of stuff girls do (which you can read about in *Girl Politics*). A guy friend is fun to have adventures with, and he can explain a lot about the boy world. *The challenge*: Other kids might tease you about "going out" and assume you're boyfriend and girlfriend. *Whatever*. Explain that you're just friends, and then ignore the comments. You and your friend-who's-a-boy should talk about the teasing and rumors so you don't start feeling weird with each other.

Having a crush on a boy — A crush is when you have a romantic feeling about a boy. Maybe you daydream about him, wondering what it would be like to be his girlfriend. Just catching a glimpse of him or saying hi to him might make you smile for hours. It's like private practice for the time when you really will fall in love with somebody. It feels exciting. *The challenge*: You find yourself mooning over somebody who doesn't notice you or is even rude to you. That can be painful, but it doesn't mean you aren't precious and wonderful. It's just one of those little emotional things that will go away quickly. If the sad feelings last for more than a day, talk to an adult you trust. It's just way too soon for you to be that affected by a boy; there is probably something else going on with you that you don't even realize.

Having a crush on an older or famous guy — It isn't unusual to have fluttery feelings about a handsome male teacher or your youth director with the great personality. Or to daydream about meeting that music star or actor or major athlete you think is amazing. In fact, it's healthy, because it's a safe way to enjoy those feelings without ever having to worry about what to do with them. Again, it's a way of mentally rehearsing for the time when you'll have a real romance. *The challenge*: Your larger-than-life crush may disappoint you by doing something unforgivable like getting married (!) or making some huge mistake that makes the news. Since you didn't have an actual relationship with this person, your bummed-out feeling will go away, but it too prepares you for the guys in your future who may let you down. They are, after all, only human.

"Going out" with a boy—At this point in your life, you really aren't going to "go" anywhere with a boy, since you can't drive and your parents are SO not going to let you start dating! But even kids in elementary school will use that phrase to let people know they are boyfriend and girlfriend and that their feelings are only for each other. Most of the time that means they pass notes or smile at each other across the room, and they will very likely "break up" before the day is over. As long as it's just a happy game, it's another one of those practice runs for the future. *The challenge*: Kids can take it too seriously (usually the girls) and get into jealous fights with each other or feel totally devastated when the "breakup" happens. It's also not healthy when girls get so wrapped up in having a "boyfriend" that they can't talk or think about anything else, and they start changing themselves to get boys to like them. In fact, that's never healthy, no matter how old you are. Since there's really no future in "going out" at this age, why complicate your life? There's too much fun to be had doing other, healthier things.

That Is SO Me!

Yeu probably already know where you are with the guy thing, so instead, let's look at how you might handle some boy-related situations. Let this "quiz" be a fun way to learn about the sometimes-weird world of dealing with males.

1. If I have a crush on a boy in my class, I
    a. tell him how I feel.
    b. ignore him so he won't know I like him.
    c. ask *my* friend to ask *his* friend if he likes me.
    d. just have fun being around him.
    e. I don't ever get crushes on boys.

Unless you answered *e*, which is perfectly fine, *d* is the best choice. Telling him how you feel (*a*) might embarrass him (or *you* if he says yuck). Ignoring him (*b*) might cheat you out of a really good friend. *Option c* will probably mean everybody in your grade will know about it within ten minutes (even if you've sworn everybody to secrecy).

2. If a boy likes me and I'm not interested in being his girlfriend (even for an hour), I
    a. don't really say yes or no and hope he'll figure it out.
    b. get my friend to tell him to back off.
    c. tell him I can't stand him so he'll leave me alone.
    d. tell him straight out that I'll be his friend but not his girlfriend.
    e. I don't think a boy has ever had a crush on me.

Unless you answered *e*, which again is perfectly healthy, *d* is the best approach. That way, you may find a really good friend, but you don't have to go through all that dramatic stuff. Hoping he'll figure it out (*a*) isn't really fair, even though it's hard to disappoint someone. Getting friends to tell him (*b*) is a little cowardly and isn't a good habit to get into. *Option c* is downright mean and SO isn't you.

continued on next page...

3. If a boy teases me and drives me nuts, I
   a. think he has a crush on me.
   b. ask my teacher to make him stop.
   c. ignore him.
   d. laugh and tease him back.
   e. Boys don't tease me.

Unless you answered *e*, which makes your life easy (!), all of the other answers are possibly right. Thinking he has a crush on you (*a*) makes sense because boys your age often tease as a way of showing they like you — go figure! Telling the teacher (*b*) is the best approach if his teasing is mean and threatening. If he's really making you uncomfortable, by all means report it to a grown-up. Ignoring him (*c*) can work, because when someone teases it's usually to get a reaction from you; if you don't give one, there's no point in his continuing. If he doesn't stop and it's interfering with your schoolwork or your security, go to *option b*. Laughing and teasing back (*d*) is a good choice if the teasing is fun and you enjoy the boy and you can join in happily and easily. This could be the start of a great friendship!

4. If all my friends like boys and they try to push me into the boy thing, I
   a. joke about it and hope they get the message, since I don't want to make them mad.
   b. say I like a boy, just to get them to leave me alone.
   c. yell at them to back off.
   d. tell them I'm not ready for boys yet.
   e. That's never happened to me.

Hopefully your answer is *e*, because friends shouldn't put each other in that kind of position. If your answer is *d*, you are right on. It's always best to be honest about how you feel. Joking about it (*a*) leaves the door open for more pushing. Saying you like a boy when you don't (*b*) is just, well, lying and could make things *way* complicated. And *option c*, though it's honest, could put your friendship in danger. There's really never any reason to scream at your friends, and that usually only happens when you let a problem go on for too long without speaking up.

IT: Since your body is yours (and God's), you have absolute authority over who touches it and how they touch it and who doesn't touch it — even if you're only eight years old. That means that if any-one — ANYONE — touches you in a way that is uncomfortable for you, especially in your private areas, tell an adult you trust _immediately_. Don't worry about whether you're going to get in trouble — you're _not_ because it isn't your fault — or that person is going to get in trouble — he (or she) _will_ and _should_, but that isn't your fault either. Even if the person threatens that you'll be hurt if you tell anyone, don't believe it. Tell anyway. That's your best protection against being touched that way again. It doesn't matter if it's a boy in your class, a relative, an adult you know, or a stranger. If someone touches you in a way you don't want to be touched, it's wrong. Report it at once.

You're Good to Go

Whether you've just begun to notice that boys can be nice, or you're full-blown boy crazy, this is a good time to decide on your "Boy Manifesto"—which is basically your statement of how you're going to behave around boys. This is a great thing to do with your Sisterhood, because you'll need each other's support in the future.

What you'll need:

this book
some scratch paper and a pencil or markers
some nice paper and a pen
advice you've gathered about boys from wise people—especially your dad. (Of all the people in your life, he knows the most about boys and about you at the same time.)

What to do:

Gather your Sisterhood.
Make a list of all the situations you could run into with the male of the species. Examples:

* a boy asking me out
* a boy teasing me for fun
* a boy teasing me to be mean
* a boy wanting to kiss me
* a boy I'm not crazy about following me around
* wanting a boyfriend when everybody else has one and I don't

Using this book and the other advice you've brought with you, discuss how you'll handle each of those situations. Write your rough ideas on scratch paper. Then write your final ideas on your nice piece of paper. For

any situation you don't know how to deal with, go to an adult and ask. Again, a father can be a great source of information here. Examples:

✦ If a boy asks me out before I'm sixteen (or whatever age is set), I will just tell him I don't date yet.
✦ If a boy teases me just for fun and it doesn't annoy me, I'll tease back.

What it tells you:

That you have a plan, so you won't be caught by surprise. That you can now relax and enjoy friendships with boys. That you know how to make good choices.

What to do now:

Show your plan to your parents, especially your dad. If they have suggestions, consider including them in your Manifesto. Then keep it where you can look at it from time to time, especially if you find yourself thinking a lot about that little leaguer that smiled at you.

That's What I'm Talkin' About!

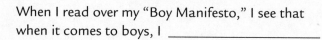

When I read over my "Boy Manifesto," I see that when it comes to boys, I _____

_____

_____

I wish boys would _____

_____

_____

When I showed him my Manifesto, my dad (or mom)

_____

_____

_____

Body
BULLIES

E very breath I take, I take in you — "
　　Fifty-one, fifty-two —
　　"*Court*-ney!"

Courtney opened her eyes and let the jump rope go slack. The music blared on in her ear. "Every step I make, I make in you ..."

"Pardon me?" she shouted to her mom, who seemed to have appeared in front of her from nowhere.

"I said turn that *off*!"

Courtney pointed to her iPod. "This?"

"Yes!"

Courtney pressed the button and blinked at her mother. "Something wrong?"

"You think?" Mom folded her arms. "When I can hear music from that little thing on the other side of the door, it's too loud."

"I have to have it loud when I'm jumping rope," Courtney said. "It helps me focus. You said you wanted me to get exercise ..."

"You're not going to be able to focus on anything if you go deaf," Mom said. "If anybody else but you can hear it, it's not good for your ears."

Courtney wasn't so sure that was true, but she nodded anyway. Parents had weird ideas sometimes.

She waited for her mom to leave so she could get back to jumping rope. She wanted to get up to 75 without stopping, and now she had to start all over. But Mom hesitated with her hand on the doorknob.

"I actually didn't stop by to nag you about your music," she said. "I just wondered if you wanted to talk about that program you had at school today."

"You mean the drug thing?" Courtney hooked the jump rope around her neck and sighed. "There's nothing to talk about. Drugs are stupid, and I'm never going to take them."

"I'm glad to hear it," Mom said. She chewed at her lip, and Courtney saw that she was actually nervous.

"Mom, it's no big deal," Courtney said. "I'm just gonna say no."

"I don't think it's that easy when the other kids are drinking at a party ..."

"Mo-om! I'm only ten years old! Nobody serves beer at sleepovers!"

"You aren't always going to be ten," Mom said. "So just remember that Dad and I are here if you want to talk about anything."

"I'm okay," Courtney said.

Her mom hugged her — for no reason Courtney could think of — and left. Courtney turned her iPod back on. Going deaf. Taking drugs. Drinking at parties. Huh. All she wanted to do was jump rope.

Here's the Deal

You too might feel like everybody is coming at you with information and warnings about stuff you haven't even thought about yet:

- taking illegal drugs;
- drinking alcohol;
- smoking;
- chewing tobacco (like you *would*!);
- listening to music at high volumes; and
- even being sexually harassed.

Like Courtney, you may be thinking, "What is the big deal? I don't even *want* to do any of those things—except maybe listen to loud music. And I'm not even sure what being sexually harassed means!"

Hopefully you *are* thinking that way, and you'll continue to believe that drugs, alcohol, and smoking are totally bad for you. Unfortunately, though, they can be very much a part of the world you're going to move into when you get to middle school, if you aren't there already. It's important that you be prepared rather than surprised. Here are some things to think about:

- Between the ages of eight and twelve, you will make key decisions about what you're going to be like and how you're going to act.
- In *many* schools, alcohol and tobacco are easy for eleven- and twelve-year-olds to get their hands on. Many kids first experiment with drinking and smoking in fifth and sixth grades, as they figure out how they're going to be and what they're going to do.
- One in every ten kids ages ten through twelve tries drugs (usually marijuana). Girls are equal in number to boys when it comes to becoming addicted (which means having to have more and more).
- The average girl your age sees 40,000 commercials a year on TV. That's 666 hours worth, and 466 of those hours show people looking and acting sexy over things like cars, deodorant, and frozen dinners! That can affect your thinking about how you're going to use your own body.

So, no, it isn't going to be as easy as "just saying no." Two things need to happen:

1. You need to have the *facts* about how bad these things are for you.
2. You need to *love* the body, mind, and spirit God has given you, just as much as you love God and other

people; so nothing can keep you from respecting and taking care of yourself.

Let's start with the facts.

Facts about Smoking:

- It causes lung disease. And that doesn't just mean sitting around with an oxygen tank when you're old. Even young people can suffer damage *now* from smoking cigarettes.
- It's *way* habit-forming. Three out of four teen girls who smoke say they've tried to quit and haven't been able to.
- A pack of cigarettes a week costs $260 a year (and most smokers go through a lot more than that).
- The nicotine in cigarettes increases the hormones that speed up your body's production of oil, which can clog your pores and cause pimples.
- It can make you four times more likely to get depressed than girls who don't smoke.
- If you're addicted to smoking and you can't have a cigarette (like during a test), your brain doesn't work as well, and your memory isn't as sharp, because you're craving the nicotine in that cigarette.
- Smoking makes it harder to exercise, because the tiny air sacs in the lungs are damaged, and you get out of breath more quickly.
- It gives you bad breath and smells up your clothes and hair and makes your teeth yellow. Just what every girl wants!

Facts about Alcohol and Drugs:

- Alcohol interferes with your growth during puberty. For example, it steals your body's zinc, which you need to grow strong bones.
- Drugs and alcohol destroy brain cells, which means you can't think as clearly or as quickly. Once those cells are dead, they don't come back to life. And in most cases, your brain doesn't make more.

People who take drugs or drink so much that they're considered drunk (they have a certain amount of alcohol in their bloodstream), risk

* doing something stupid and making fools of themselves in front of other people.
* getting physically hurt.
* being influenced to do things they wouldn't dream of doing when they weren't drunk.
* losing friends.
* getting into trouble not only with parents but with police.
* having their stuff stolen or broken.
* arguing or fighting with people (and possibly being injured).
* throwing up.
* becoming unconscious.
* even dying (from too much alcohol in a small, young body—and "too much" is not a lot).

So, if all that stuff is obviously bad for you, why does anybody do it? Why don't kids just say no?

It sounds simple, but there are ideas and thoughts that come with—you guessed it—puberty that can make it hard to stay away from drugs, alcohol, and tobacco. It's natural at your age to

want to fit in, be included, and be liked.

want to do the fun things the other kids are doing.

want to feel more grown-up.

want to try new things.

look up to older kids and role models to show you how to act.

realize it's *your* body and *you* have control over it (and to think, "So why can't I do whatever I want with it?").

figure out it's one of the few things you *do* have control over, when other people are controlling your behavior and your time and where you live.

Think about these situations:

ALL the girls at the sleepover are going to try half a glass of somebody's dad's wine, just to see what it tastes and feels like. These are the girls you hang out with all the time. There's nobody else to be with at school. You'll be all alone in the cafeteria, and on the playground ...

At home, your parents treat you like *such* a baby. Your best friend's big sister offers you a cigarette, telling you that you're way more mature than even some of her friends. Just for a minute you'd like to feel grown-up ...

That boy all your friends are giggling about—the most popular kid in the whole class—has marijuana in his backpack, and you see it. If you tell on him, everybody is going to be mad at you. Your life will be over—or it might as well be ...

It isn't as easy as it sounds, is it? That's why it's a good thing we've got God.

GOT GOD?

The reason friends are so important to you right now is because God set it up that way. It's part of the natural growing-up process for you to start to turn your attention away from your family and focus it on your friends. You will someday move out of your parents' house completely to have your own life, and right now you are slowly learning how.

Your friends, then, are giving you the safe, secure feeling of belonging that came totally from your family when you were a small girl. But what if suddenly you won't belong if you don't do what your friends are doing? What if they're making choices you know aren't right or healthy? What if you wind up alone and out-cast and never have friends again and everyone hates you and—

Okay, you can stop right there, because you *know* that last one isn't going to happen! The other things can, though, and it hurts when they do. But isn't it just like God to have answers for us?

> Blessed are those who are persecuted because of righteousness, for theirs is the kingdom of heaven.
>
> —MATTHEW 5:10

God knows what it's like to be made fun of and pushed aside because you won't go along with the group. He not only under-stands, he gives you a deep feeling of goodness, which at the end of the day feels a lot better than knowing you gave in.

> Do not envy wicked men [or girls], do not desire their company; for their hearts plot violence, and their lips talk about making trouble.
>
> —PROVERBS 24:1-2

It can be painful, but some friendships do break up in these tween years over different ideas about what's right and what's wrong. The girls you always played dolls and swam and went to Brownies with may make choices about their lives that you can't agree with. Then it's time to end the friendship. Go ahead and cry, and then be glad you're free from things that are only going to get you into trouble.

[Peter said,] "Save yourselves from this corrupt generation." ... All the believers were together and had everything in common.... Every day they continued to meet together.... They broke bread in their homes and ate together with glad and sincere hearts, praising God and enjoying the favor of all the people.

– ACTS 2:40, 44, 46 - 47

Gather new friends, other girls (and even boys) who are making healthy decisions about their lives. Get together to talk about how you're going to resist the bad stuff and fill your time with *great* stuff. Hang out with kids who love God the way you do.

It is God's will ... that each of you should learn to control his [or her] own body in a way that is holy and honorable.... For God did not call us to be impure, but to live a holy life. Therefore, he who rejects this instruction does not reject man but God, who gives you his Holy Spirit.

– 1 THESSALONIANS 4:3 - 4, 7 - 8

Remember that taking care of your temple is more important than your social life. We're talking about your body, the one you share with God. Appreciate and give dignity to it. If you reject your body by abusing it, you reject God.

Clear enough?

IT: You really can experience hearing loss from having your iPod or MP3 player cranked up too high. Experts say one hour on a portable player at sixty percent of the volume is pretty safe. Ask someone to show you what level that is on yours.

That Is SO Me!

Imagine that you and your friends are at one of your houses and you're going to watch a movie together. There are bunches to choose from. The girl's mom has set out snacks in the kitchen for you, and both parents have gone to bed. Circle *all* the things below that you would do. Remember—be honest!

Pick the movie.

Turn the movie off if it's lame.

Announce you're hungry.

Keep watching as long as everyone else does.

Watch what the group decides.

Turn the movie off if it has violence or bad language.

Make sure the kitchen isn't left messy.

Start the movie.

See what's in the pantry to eat.

See if there's an R-rated movie.

Go do something else if the movie's lame.

Join in the fun of everyone eating the same thing.

Now find all your choices in the lists below. You will probably see yourself in more than one because you're a complex human being. Just let the lists tell you how your choices sometimes serve you well and sometimes don't. What you discover about yourself can help prepare you for bigger choices that can have more serious results.

Rule Maker

Pick the movie.
Announce you're hungry.
Turn the movie off if it's lame.

You're a strong person in your group. You're often the one who decides what's going to happen and how things are going to be done. You can use that to influence your friends to make fun, not trouble. Just be careful not to be too B-O-S-S-Y.

Rule Keeper

Start the movie.

Make sure the kitchen isn't left messy.

Turn the movie off if it has violence or bad language.

You don't make the rules, but you know them and you make sure everybody else does too. Even if they don't stick to them, you will. Keep doing that when it comes to the tough decisions. Just remember that you're not responsible for other people's choices, so you don't always have to be the watchdog.

Rule Follower

Watch what the group decides.

Join in the fun of everyone eating the same thing.

Keep watching as long as everyone else does.

You're an easy person to get along with, and you keep things calm in your group of friends by being agreeable. It's good to be unselfish, but be careful not to follow the group's "rules" if they aren't good ones. Stand up for what's right when you need to.

Rule Breaker

See if there's an R-rated movie.

See what's in the pantry to eat.

Go do something else if the movie is lame.

You are an independent person, and you like to see what all the possibilities are. You aren't afraid to take risks or see how far the rules can be pushed (just in case they're lame rules). Use your adventurous spirit to question your friends when they all just want to go along with the crowd—in the wrong direction. Be sure your choices are brave, not just rebellious.

You're Good to Go

 This is a good time to get your Sisterhood together and make a plan for dealing with the "Body Bullies" that are sure to come your way. Making good choices is so much easier when you can do it together.

What you'll need:

your group, of course
pencil and paper
this book
a computer, or some special paper and pens or markers

What to do:

Pray together that God will show you exactly the right things to decide.

Go through this chapter together and make a list of the issues you'll probably face (or maybe already do). Your list would include things like drinking, smoking, listening to too-loud music, and so on. Leave a few lines between each one.

Talk about each issue and decide

- your attitude about it. (Is it wrong? Unhealthy? Disgusting?)
- how you'll resist it. (Run the other way? Refuse to hang out with people who do it? Call each other when you're tempted?)
- how you'll fight it in your world. (Turn in kids who do it? Make T-shirts with slogans? Befriend girls who are feeling pressured?)

Type up your plan on a computer and print copies for everyone in your Sisterhood, or let each person write out and decorate her own copy while you talk (and snack, of course!).

What it tells you:

- That you are mature enough to know how a real "grown-up" makes decisions.
- That you can take a stand instead of hoping things don't happen to you.
- That you aren't alone in facing the hard things that may lie ahead. You have God and your friends.
- That it's more fun to be healthy with your friends than to mess up your lives together.

What to do now:

It's not easy, but it *is* simple. Just study your plan and go out there and do it. Remember, God is right there with you.

That's What I'm Talkin' About!

Now that my friends and I have a plan, I feel better about

_____

_____

_____

We actually used it when _____

_____

_____

_____

I will probably have to use it because _____

_____

_____

_____

chapter nine

Mini-
WOMAN

When the doorbell rang, Courtney didn't answer it right away. She took one more look around the family room. The table was practically groaning with all the food on it — a huge bowl of fresh fruit, a plate overflowing with raw, cut-up veggies, and a platter of whole-wheat crackers and slices of turkey and cheese.

Music danced over the room. Her friends' favorites were stacked beside the CD player, which was set at volume six.

All the furniture was pushed back against the walls so there was plenty of room for practicing cheers and making up dances … and for spreading out sleeping bags when they finally dropped.

Everything was perfect, including the fact that Dad had taken Sam and Will to Grandma's for the night. They could actually have girl talk without worrying about being spied on — or worse.

The bell rang again, and Courtney flew to the door to let in Anna, Kayla, and Sydney. It was amazing how fast the family room filled up with giggling and hugging and the dumping of bags. Courtney couldn't stop grinning.

"Look at all this food," Anna said.

Sydney peered over her shoulder. "No chips?"

"Court, can I have a soda?" Kayla said.

Courtney had expected that. She just smiled and said, "How about some juice?"

They all stared at her and blinked. Then Sydney shrugged and dove for the CD player, which she hiked up to volume nine.

"I love this song!" she said.

"What?" Kayla said.

Anna poked Courtney. "Turn it down. I wanna tell you guys something."

Kayla punched the Off button, and the girls dropped to the floor in a circle. Anna's eyes were wide and full of information.

"My cousin was here this week — you know, the one who's fifteen and way mature — "

They all nodded. Courtney remembered this cousin. She had a body like a model, and she always smelled good.

"Anyway," Anna went on, "she told me everything we need to know about getting your period. Stuff we never even thought about."

Courtney doubted that. Her mom had been answering her questions for weeks now. What more could there be to know?

"Like what?" Kayla said to Anna.

Sydney appeared to be holding her breath.

"Well ..." Anna sat up importantly. "Your breasts can, like, double in size right before you start."

"No way!" Sydney said.

That was what Courtney was thinking.

"You need to have two different size bras."

"Nuh-uh!" Sydney and Kayla said together.

"And if you're on your period, don't go to the dentist because he'll totally be able to tell. Boys can too. It's something about your breath."

"Like Ferris Fox would know?" Kayla said. Her eyes were popping. "How?"

"Oh, and she also said — "

"Stop," Courtney said.

Anna looked at Courtney, her mouth still forming her next word. Kayla and Sydney waited. Courtney took a deep breath and spoke ...

After you've read this chapter, you'll have a chance to write the ending for Courtney in "That's What I'm Talkin' About!" She's learned a lot while you've been reading this book, and we hope you have too. Let's review before you — and Courtney — set everybody straight.

In the first chapters of Genesis, when you read the story of how God made the world, you can't help seeing what an imagination God has.

Darkness. Light. Sky. Ground. Seas. Every kind of plant, tree, and seed. Stars. Seasons. Sun. Water teeming with living creatures.

Now, *that's* creative.

And when God created people, he gave the special touch that goes beyond *our* imagination:

> God created man in his own image,
> in the image of God he created him;
> male and female he created them.
> — GENESIS 1:27

Can you even begin to *think* about the care that went into creating a person? A woman? Puberty alone boggles the mind with all its details and the way everything works together to turn you into a woman.

And what about the way each of us is different? No two of us are exactly alike in body (or any other way). We are each exactly the way God meant for us to be. We know that from the next part of the verse:

God blessed them.
—GENESIS 1:28

Besides just being awesome, all of that tells you three things:

1. You can have confidence that God gave you exactly the body you're supposed to have.
2. You really have to love that body.
3. You are responsible for taking care of it.

There is no comparing in that job description—no, "I wish I were as skinny as Miss Thing," or "I'm glad I have breasts now, not like Little Flat Chest over there."

There is no self-hate mentioned there—no, "I'm so fat I'm going to starve myself," or "Who cares if I exercise? I'm just a blob anyway."

And do you see any shoving the job off on somebody else? No—there's no, "I can't help it if the school cafeteria only serves pizza," or "My family members aren't athletes. We just like to watch TV."

It's pretty clear. Love that precious body. Be sure it's totally you. Take the best care of it that you can. God says so.

That Is SO Me!

I n this book, you've read about what it looks like to love and take care of your body. There's a lot to it—no doubt about that—especially during this time of your life when it can look and feel like a different body every day! Let's just see how you're doing—so you can give yourself a hug—and what you might want to work on next—so you can keep growing into the marvelous young woman God made you to be.

Put a check mark next to each of the things you've done or are doing for body care.

____ I understand what's happening or is about to happen inside my body (puberty).

____ I have a comfortable bra or know what size I wear and what kind I'd like to try.

____ I know I'm right where I should be—not "ahead" or "behind" in my development.

____ I have my supplies ready for when I start my first or next period.

____ I have a Personal Fitness Plan to make sure I get enough exercise.

____ I eat healthy, according to the food pyramid.

____ I get at least eight hours of sleep every night.

____ I refuse to "go on a diet" unless my doctor says I need to.

____ I drink at least eight glasses of water a day.

____ I take a bath or shower every day.

____ I wear clean clothes every day.

____ I use a deodorant or antiperspirant if I need to.

____ I have a Boy Manifesto.

____ I have a plan for dealing with "Body Bullies."

____ I have a Sisterhood to go through puberty with.

____ I go to a trusted adult with problems that bother or upset me.

You're Good to Go

Go back to the beginning of this chapter and read about Courtney again.

Knowing all that you and Courtney have learned after reading this book, decide what Courtney would say to her friends—not only about their misinformation on puberty, but also about the other body mistakes they've been making since they walked through the door. Think about how she'll say it and how she'll feel.

Now write the story ending, just the way you see and hear it.

That's What I'm Talkin' About!

Since I've started taking better care of my body, I can tell that_____

_____

_____

Someone else said he/she noticed a good change in me. _____

_____

_____

I feel like God's temple because _____

_____

_____

_____

faiThGirLz!
the beauty of believing

The Skin You're In

Discovering True Beauty

Previously titled Beauty Lab

Nancy Rue

chapter one

You've Got It
GOIN' ON

The morning Betsy Honeycutt turned eleven, she took a big ol' long look in the mirror, and she didn't like what she saw.

That was pretty weird, since she had seen the very same face the day before (and the day before that and the day before — well, you get the idea), and she hadn't thought much about her freckles or her blue eyes or her honey-brown bob one way or the other. Yesterday she was just Betsy. But today — yikes!

Has my nose always been that long? she thought. *Gross! It looks like a fishhook!*

And what about my eyes? They've gotten closer together — I know they have!

Betsy watched her upper lip curl. Her very thin lip — not plump and luscious like the girls' mouths in the magazines that she'd just fanned across her bed. In fact, there was nothing about her that was even remotely like a model, or, come to think of it, like any of the girls at school that everybody was imitating. She narrowed her eyes at her reflection.

Her hair wasn't long and shiny and thick like Madison's.

Her teeth weren't perfectly white and straight like Taylor's.

And where in the *world* had that *zit* come from? Ashleigh didn't have *zits!*

Betsy gasped right out loud and shoved her face closer to the mirror. It was a pimple between her eyebrows, all right, red and ugly and growing bigger by the millisecond.

She stepped back, hoping it wouldn't look so hideous from farther away, but it was like there was a spotlight shining on it so the entire world could check it out. And not only that, but now she could see her whole self in all her glory.

"Uh, I am *so not* glorious," Betsy said.

The girl in the mirror looked to her like a shapeless blob, dressed in a too-small T-shirt and a too-big pair of shorts that revealed legs hairier than her cocker spaniel's. When she put her hand up to her mouth in disgust, all she saw was the froggy green nail polish she'd put on at last week's sleepover and had been steadily gnawing away at ever since.

"And this is before I turned the lights on," Betsy told the stranger-self. "EWWWWW!"

She turned away from the mirror and looked down at the clear-skinned faces of the perfect girls on the magazine covers. *Will I ever be that pretty?* she thought.

She didn't see how the answer could ever be yes.

Which of these comes closest to what you were you
thinking as you read Betsy's story?

    ___ I don't get it. I hardly ever hang out looking in the
    mirror.
    ___ Um, I kind of like what I see when I look in the mirror.
    ___ Hello-o! I know exactly how she feels!

Just about every girl between the ages of eight and twelve
starts to think—at least a little bit—about the way she looks. But
did you know that the minute you're aware that your appearance
is a big part of yourself, you're on a journey?

It can be a lifetime of visits to the mirror where you can
always find something *wrong*. Or ... it can be an adventure of
discovering the true, absolute, no-denying-it beauty that every girl
has—that *you* have.

The choice is pretty much a no-brainer, which is why you have
this book in your hand. This book is here to help you set out on
the way-fun path to finding your beautiful self. And not just the
hair-and-skin-and-clothes outside self, but the unique, one-of-a-
kind inside you, which is where real beauty comes from. More on
that later.

Before you begin the adventure, it's good to know where
you are right now. Write in the space on the next page what you
would say to Betsy if you were in her bedroom, watching her
suffer in front of the mirror. Look back at what you checked off
above to help you. There are no right or wrong answers, so be
free and real as you write. If, as you read on in this book, you
change your mind about what you want to say to Betsy, you'll
have a chance to express that when we get to the end.

Dear Betsy...

When it comes to thinking about the way you look, you're probably somewhere between "What's a mirror?" and "I want to put a bag over my head!" Whatever you think about your beauty, chances are you've gotten some ideas about what beautiful is by looking around and listening. Maybe you've heard things like this:

> "She's so thin. I wish I looked like her."
> "Her skin is perfect. Look at that! I bet she's never had a pimple."
> "Long blonde hair and big blue eyes—now *that's* what I'm talking about."
> "Train to be a model or just look like one! Call now! Operators are standing by!"

To hear people talk, you'd think the only girls who could be considered beautiful are pencil skinny with flawless complexions, long blonde hair, and big blue eyes; and they dress only in the trends that just started this morning. But think about all the girls and women you know that you consider beautiful. Do they all look like that?

What about

✿ your best friend?
✿ your favorite female teacher?
✿ your cool aunt, the cousin you want to be like, and your mom?
✿ And, hey—what about *you*?

Yeah, you. If you counted up all the people who like you and love you, you'd run out of fingers. Ask any one of them if he or she thinks you're a beautiful person, and you'll hear, "Honey, you're drop-dead gorgeous," or something like that.

The point is, no matter what people say about being beautiful, when you get right down to it, the ones who count in your life know real, true, unique beauty when they see it. So how do girls get the idea that they have to look like the cover girl on *Seventeen* to be pretty?

Simple.

From the media. That's TV, movies, billboards, magazines—anything that a lot of people see. The beauties there are all different, but they have one thing in common:

(Important Thing):

Don't ask a boy younger than twenty-five. He can't handle questions like that yet. You're sure to get a variation of, "Yeah, if you like baboons," which probably means he likes you—but don't even go there.

they're perfect. Oops—wait. They *look* perfect. But if you met one of them outside the studio, you'd see right away that she has flaws just like everybody else: A piece of hair that won't stay out of her eye; the retainer she just popped in; maybe even a zit—yikes! You don't see those things in an ad or on the movie screen because (1) a team of makeup artists, personal trainers, and wardrobe consultants were all over her before she went before the camera, and (2) film editors can do amazing things with digital enhancing, just the way you can in Photoshop. A couple of clicks and that piece of flyaway hair or that enormous pimple disappears. The eyes are darker. The dress fits better. Get it? A famous model named Cindy Crawford once said, "Even I don't wake up looking like Cindy Crawford."

From models. You may have seen a professional model in person, and she did look pretty perfect to you. There wasn't an ounce of fat on her body! Before you consider yourself a hippo because at ten years old you weigh more than she does at twenty, remember this: A girl who becomes a model tends to be naturally thin and very tall to begin with. Then it becomes part of her job to keep her weight low so the curves of her body don't take attention away from the clothes she's modeling. Many models diet constantly, practically living on water and celery, and they work out daily for hours on end. Don't even think about doing that. You have healthy growing to do.

From what boys say. Like you care, right? But you can't help hearing them because they're so loud. They're going through their own stuff right now, so a lot of them think they have to be funny all the time. You've probably noticed that what boys consider funny is different from what cracks up you and your friends. They think it's hilarious to call you Tinsel Teeth because you just got braces or to swat at cooties when you stand next to them. Even though you know they're just being absurd little creeps, you can get your feelings hurt. Give them a few years. They'll get nicer. Meanwhile, don't take beauty tips from them.

By comparing yourself to the "cool" girls. Sometime in elementary school, it starts to become obvious that some girls are considered "cooler" than others. We don't know who decides that. Unfortunately, it just happens. Because the cool girls get a lot of attention and have a bunch of friends, almost everybody wants to be like them. And then the comparing starts:

- "Her hair is blonder (or darker) than mine."
- "Her eyes are bigger (or bluer or sparklier) than mine."
- "My clothes aren't as cute as hers."
- "She doesn't have to wear stupid braces like I do."

It can be pretty tempting to try to change yourself to be more like the cool girl. Or you may dislike the cool girl because seeing her makes you feel so bad about yourself. Or—if you happen to be a cool girl—you may work overtime trying to *stay* cool. None of that is any fun. And none of it makes you beautiful. It makes you worried, unhappy, and resentful—but not beautiful.

Besides, here's the deal—and if you get nothing else from this book, get this—YOU ARE ALREADY BEAUTIFUL!!!! Maybe on the outside you haven't "grown into yourself" yet. Maybe you haven't learned to make the most of what you have. Maybe you have hard stuff going on in your life that keeps you from really showing your beauty. But you were made to be a beautiful person. She's in there. After all, God doesn't make ugly. Okay, so maybe roaches are ugly ... but the boy roaches think they're kinda cute.

You were made to be your unique, shining, beautiful, true self. This journey you're on is about finding that self and letting her shine.

Who says? Well, hello-o ...

Sophie Series
Written by Nancy Rue

Meet Sophie LaCroix, a creative soul who's destined to become a great film director someday. But many times her overactive imagination gets her in trouble!

Check out the other books in the series!

Book 1: Sophie's World
IBSN: 978-0-310-70756-1

Book 7: Sophie's Friendship Fiasco
ISBN: 978-0-310-71842-0

Book 2: Sophie's Secret
ISBN: 978-0-310-70757-8

Book 8: Sophie and the New Girl
ISBN: 978-0-310-71843-7

Book 3: Sophie Under Pressure
ISBN: 978-0-310-71840-6

Book 9: Sophie Flakes Out
ISBN: 978-0-310-71024-0

Book 4: Sophie Steps Up
ISBN: 978-0-310-71841-3

Book 10: Sophie Loves Jimmy
ISBN: 978-0-310-71025-7

Book 5: Sophie's First Dance
ISBN: 978-0-310-70760-8

Book 11: Sophie's Drama
ISBN: 978-0-310-71844-4

Book 6: Sophie's Stormy Summer
ISBN: 978-0-310-70761-5

Book 12: Sophie Gets Real
ISBN: 978-0-310-71845-1

Nonfiction

Everybody Tells Me to Be Myself but I Don't Know Who I Am

ISBN 978-0-310-71295-4

This addition to the Faithgirlz! line helps girls face the challenges of being their true selves with fun activities, interactive text, and insightful tips.

Girl Politics

ISBN 978-0-310-71296-1

Parents and kids alike may think that getting teased or arguing with friends is just part of growing up, but where is the line between normal kid stuff and harmful behavior? This book is a guide for girls on how to deal with girl politics, God-style.

The Skin You're In

ISBN 978-0-310-71999-1

Beauty tips and the secret of true inner beauty are revealed in this interactive, inspirational, fun addition to the Faithgirlz! line.

Body Talk

ISBN 978-0-310-71275-6

In a world where bodies are commodities, girls are under more pressure at younger ages. This book is a fun and God-centered way to give girls the facts and self-confidence they need as they mature into young women.

Available now at your local bookstore!
Visit www.faithgirlz.com, it's the place for girls ages 9-12.

Devotions

No Boys Allowed Devotions for Girls

Softcover • ISBN 9780310707189

This short, ninety-day devotional for girls ages 10 and up is written in an upbeat, lively, funny, and tween-friendly way, incorporating the graphic, fast-moving feel of a teen magazine.

Girlz Rock Devotions for You

Softcover • ISBN 9780310708995

In this ninety-day devotional, devotions like "Who Am I?" help pave the spiritual walk of life, and the "Girl Talk" feature poses questions that really bring each message home. No matter how bad things get, you can always count on God.

Chick Chat More Devotions for Girls

Softcover • ISBN 9780310711438

This ninety-day devotional brings the Bible right into your world and offers lots to learn and think about.

Shine On, Girl! Devotions to Keep You Sparkling

Softcover • ISBN 9780310711445

This ninety-day devotional will "totally" help teen girls connect with God, as well as learn his will for their lives.

Available now at your local bookstore!
Visit www.faithgirlz.com, it's the place for girls ages 9-12.

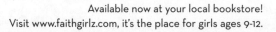

faiThGirLz!
the beauty of believing

Bibles

Every girl wants to know she's totally unique and special. This Bible says that with Faithgirlz! sparkle! Now girls can grow closer to God as they discover the journey of a lifetime, in their language, for their world.

The NIV Faithgirlz! Bible

Hardcover
ISBN 978-0-310-71581-8

Softcover
ISBN 978-0-310-71582-5

The NIV Faithgirlz! Bible

Italian Duo-Tone™
ISBN 978-0-310-71583-2

The NIV Faithgirlz! Backpack Bible

Periwinkle
Italian Duo-Tone™
ISBN 978-0-310-71012-7

Available now at your local bookstore!
Visit www.faithgirlz.com, it's the place for girls ages 9-12.